Biblical
Church Unity

Biblical
Church Unity

John Hooper

BOOKS
Plas Gwyn, Trelawnyd, LL18 6DT
ISBN 0 9523041 2 0

Biblical Church Unity

First published in Great Britain in 1998
by K & M Books

© John Hooper 1998

ISBN 0 9523041 2 0

An earlier version of this material has appeared in
the Protestant Reformed Theological Journal.
Vol XXXI. No . November 1997 ISSN: 1070-8138

BOOKS

Plas Gwyn, Trelawnyd, LL18 6DT

Typset and printed by

Tentmaker Publications

Stoke-on-Trent

Contents

3

Behold, how good and how pleasant it is
for brethren to dwell together in unity!
It is like the precious ointment upon the head,
that ran down the beard, even Aaron's beard:
that went down to the skirts of his garments;
as the dew of Hermon,
and as the dew that descended upon the mountains of Zion:
for there the LORD commanded the blessing,
even life for evermore.

Psalm 133

Introduction

The expression 'church unity' is viewed by many Evangelical and Reformed people today with understandable suspicion. Being a term that is almost exclusively associated with the ecumenical movement, it conjures up pictures of main-line denominations striving to bury their differences and merging to form ever larger 'church' organizations. One can see as the ultimate end of this movement reunion of the nominal Protestant churches with Rome, and the formation of a one-world church having the Pope at its head. Certainly all talk of church unity in this sense is off the agenda for Christians and churches who seek to be governed by the Word of God.

There is a danger, however, that in our eagerness to condemn the false we also overlook the true. It may be that we even condemn the true with the false. As a reaction against ecumenism the tendency very often is for Evangelical churches to adopt a position of independence, eschewing formal ties with other churches of like mind.

In addition to those churches that have been historically independent, the last thirty or so years have seen many ministers and churches in the United Kingdom withdrawing from the main denominations over doctrinal issues, and maintaining an independent existence. For some this has involved paying a high material price. One can sympathize with their reluctance to become embroiled again in denominational issues. Their fears of theological compromise, that is so much a part of main-line denominational life, are perfectly understandable. But the question arises, do the results of this surge in Independency—and a radical Independency at that, which the Independents of old would hardly recognize—really commend it as a God-honouring alternative? And more to the point, is it really Biblical?

It is sad, yet true to say, that as the thinking Christian takes a step back to survey the Evangelical/Reformed church scene in Britain today, all he sees is confusion. He sees a hotchpotch of churches and 'fellowships', each loudly claiming loyalty to the Scriptures, yet each

7

going its own way and doing its own thing. Surely the time has come for someone to ask whether this situation brings glory to God? Is this what Paul really means by decency and order? Is this the situation that prevailed in the days of the early church as, led by the Holy Spirit, the apostles established churches throughout Asia Minor and Europe?

It seems to me that while we have been quick to condemn the false unity of the ecumenical movement, and rightly so, we have been strangely silent in promoting the true unity revealed in the Scriptures. This study is an attempt to break that silence and to present what I am increasingly convinced is the Biblical teaching on the unity of the church, particularly as that unity is expressed in her life and government. May it encourage the thoughtful reader to search the Scriptures for himself, and prayerfully consider the issues with a view to applying them to our desperately needy times.

I.

The Principle
of Biblical Church Unity

In essence the church is a perfect unity. The Bible teaches us that this is true despite all the apparent evidence to the contrary. Whatever we may see around us and experience in our own lives of divisions and strife amongst Christians and churches, it remains ever true that the church of Jesus Christ is one. She is made up of the elect children of God, each foreknown and chosen in Christ before the foundation of the world, from every nation, tribe and tongue, of every generation, redeemed and gathered together into one. In His electing work God did not choose for Himself a disordered rag-bag of individuals, He chose a church, a single, structured, living organism to be understood spiritually as one united whole, in Christ.

Scripture uses many vivid figures of speech to illustrate this truth and bring it home to us clearly. The church is described as one flock of many sheep, a house, a temple of many stones fitly framed together (cf. John 10:16; I Pet. 2; Eph. 2:11-22; Eph. 4:15,16). Above all she is the glorious body of Christ, one entire, perfect body comprised of many members, each having his proper place and rôle in the body, together constituting one organic whole: 'For as the body is one, and hath many members, and all the members of that one body, being many, are one body: so also is Christ...' (I Cor. 12:12ff.; see also Rom. 12:4,5; I Cor. 10:17; Gal. 3:28; Eph. 1:22,23; Eph. 4:4; Eph. 5:30).

The subject of this booklet, then, is the unity of Christ, and His is a perfect, unblemished unity that cannot be divided (I Cor. 1:13).

Be of one mind

This being the case, we must emphasize, as does Scripture itself, that the unity of Christ's body is a unity that must be visibly expressed on

9

earth. Again and again the Holy Spirit, through the apostolic writers, exhorts the people of God to unity.

News had evidently reached Paul that there were divisions at Corinth: '...it hath been declared unto me of you, my brethren,... that there are contentions among you.' He condemns this open warfare between brethren as carnality. They were still babes in Christ, or at least behaving as babes. He continues, 'Now I beseech you, brethren, by the name of our Lord Jesus Christ, that ye all speak the same thing, and that there be no divisions among you; but that ye be perfectly joined together in the same mind and in the same judgment' (I Cor. 1:11,10). Again, as he takes leave of them in his second letter, Paul reminds them of their calling: 'Finally, brethren, farewell. Be perfect, be of good comfort, be of one mind, live in peace; and the God of love and peace shall be with you' (II Cor. 13:11).

Writing to the Philippians, Paul tells them of the joy they bring to his soul, but it is a joy that is as yet incomplete. He admonishes them, in order that his joy might attain its full measure, 'that ye be like minded, having the same love, being of one accord, of one mind' (Phil. 2:2).

Thus Paul was at pains to promote unity and to encourage the saints to be of one mind and to live at peace with one another. The local church was not to be a place of discord and dissent but of peace, brotherly love, and unity. Believers were to be 'kindly affectioned one to another with brotherly love' (Rom. 12:10). 'For God is not the author of confusion, but of peace, as in all churches of the saints' (I Cor. 14:33). Peace is a fruit of the Spirit (Gal. 5:22) and ought to pervade all His gathered churches. 'Let the peace of God rule in your hearts, to the which also ye are called in one body' (Col. 3:15).

But our subject is not primarily the unity of the local church. We will take that as understood. What we need to grasp is that the calls for unity which the apostle made, while certainly addressed to specific historic local churches, were also intended for a far wider audience. The unity the Lord requires is a unity that reaches far beyond the walls of the church local.

It is this aspect of truth, so commonly abused, neglected, ignored, or denied, that we want to examine here.

The Scope of the Command

The epistles, and hence their exhortations to unity, were not always addressed to individual local congregations. When Peter wrote, 'be ye all of one mind' (I Pet. 3:8), it was not to one local church in one town but to all the scattered saints of Asia Minor, an area covering many thousands of square miles (I Pet. 1:1). Likewise, when Paul wrote 'be of one mind', it was to 'the church of God which is at Corinth, with all the saints which are in all Achaia' (II Cor. 13:11; 1:1), Achaia being a province of Greece covering the whole of the southern half of the country. A church which most certainly would have been included in this salutation, together with that at Corinth, was the one at Cenchrea (Rom. 16:1). The churches in that part of the world were not just to be at one internally but also with each other.

Similarly the Galatian letter had a regional application. Galatia covered a large central area of what is now Turkey and was blessed with a number of local churches. This explains why Paul addressed his letter to 'the churches of Galatia' (Gal. 1:1; note the plural). Again, when he writes to the Corinthian believers, concerning the collection of alms, he says, 'as I have given order to the churches of Galatia, even so do ye' (I Cor 16:1).

The Colossian letter too was written for more than one congregation. We know that in the neighbourhood of Colosse both Philemon and Nymphas had churches meeting in their homes (cf. Philm. 2 and Col. 4:9; 4:15). Furthermore, this letter was to be taken to the nearby city of Laodicea and there 'read also in the church of the Laodiceans'. In return the Colossians were to 'likewise read the epistle from Laodicea' (Col. 4:16).

We may broaden the scope still further because, in writing his first letter to the Corinthians, Paul was addressing 'all that in every place call upon the name of Jesus Christ our Lord' (I Cor. 1:2). His Ephesian letter too is addressed generally to 'the faithful in Christ Jesus' (Eph. 1:1).

We can draw from these Scriptures the conclusion that unity was to be present not only *within* the churches of the New Testament, but also *amongst* them. All who everywhere called upon the name of Jesus Christ at that time were to speak the same thing and be of one mind, without strife or division. It was a responsibility placed upon the people of God generally, wherever they were to be found.

But there is a still wider application. Those exhortations to unity were not given to churches of just one age and generation but to the entire New Testament church. They are for every subsequent generation. The letters of Paul and the other apostles have been bound together by the Holy Spirit into one inspired sacred volume. Together with the writings of the prophets (cf. Eph. 2:20), they have been sent to all the churches of every succeeding generation, to the four corners of the earth. They are not bound by time or space. The appeals for unity, therefore, are directed toward us too!

Yes, we in our day have a responsibility to the Head of the church to ensure that there are no divisions and schisms within His body but that all are of the same mind, united with a unity that extends beyond the walls of our own local church to embrace all who in every place call upon the name of Jesus Christ our Lord. That is a heavy responsibility, but to ignore it is most certainly to live in disobedience to our common Lord.

Perhaps at this point someone raises the objection that it is not being realistic to expect all believers to dwell together in unity. It is impossible to fulfil. It is difficult enough to achieve unity in one local church, and a small one at that, let alone among a number of churches. And as for all churches being united together, that is pure fantasy.

To a certain extent, that is quite true. There is a diversity in the church, stemming from the huge variety of cultures, languages, and personalities that are represented among her members. This is the way it is meant to be. The Word of God teaches us that the church is catholic, i.e., universal, composed of all kinds of people whom God gathers together into one for His own glory (cf. Gal. 3:28; Eph. 1:4-12; Rom. 10:12,13). The great multitude that John saw in front of the throne and the Lamb were 'of all nations, and kindreds, and people, and tongues' (Rev. 7:9).

But in their warnings against disunity the apostles are not referring to this kind of healthy diversity. They are writing against differences in doctrine and practice, differences that are the result of failure to understand, believe, and obey God's Word. They are referring to differences that stem from the church's *sin*.

For as long as there is sin there will be divisions, and realistically these sinful divisions can never be dispelled until sin itself is finally destroyed. But we are not to tolerate them. Still we are commanded to be of one mind.

The apostles' exhortations are not meant to be realistic: they are idealistic. They establish a principle. They are what *God* says and are made from His perspective. They do not make allowances for the fact that churches are made up of people who are still sinners and still prone to pride, disputing, strife, jealousy, and so on. They set out the ultimate standard, even though that standard can never be met here on earth. They show us the perfect way in which we should strive to walk. They show us the goal that we are to desire with all our heart and work for with all our strength.

That is how it is with all of God's commands. They present us with our moral obligations. The fact that we are not able to live out a principle does not invalidate that principle or release us from its obligation. We cannot live a single hour without sinning, but still God says, 'Be ye holy for I am holy.' Likewise He still says, 'Be ye all of one mind.' It is a command based upon the incontrovertible principle that the church of Jesus Christ is one. The only reason that she is not one and cannot be one in this world is the sinful, proud independence of us, her members.

Only in the sinless perfection of heaven, when God will have finally gathered together in one all things in Christ (Eph. 1:10), will our desires be fulfilled and the ideal will become glorious reality. Only then, when we are free from sin, shall we be perfectly united and love one another as we should. Only then will the body of Christ know perfect unity within herself and with her Head, and what is true now in principle will be true also in experience.

But even so, we may, we should, experience something of that heavenly unity here upon earth. We have been born again. God has given us not only His commands but He has also given us His Spirit. This means that, despite our fallen nature, with the command and responsibility comes also the ability to obey. By the Spirit of God we are able to know in some small measure, as a foretaste of heaven, the unity of His church. Hence it is called 'the unity of the Spirit' (Eph. 4:3). It is a unity that is produced and imparted by the Holy Spirit of

Christ. He brings forth from our hearts and lives the fruit of love, joy, peace etc. (Gal. 5:22,23), so that even Jews and Gentiles are brought together in the bond of peace. It is for this unity that we are to strive.

Unity in Operation

The unity of the Spirit is not merely an abstract idea that cannot be experienced, but is a principle that manifests itself in practical, tangible ways. The reader of the book of Acts and the letters of the apostles ought not fail to notice this. The very fact that the epistles were not always addressed to individual congregations but in some cases to regional groups of churches is itself evidence of unity at work.

When the inevitable divisions arose amongst churches, such as those in Achaia, they were dealt with promptly. Churches were separated geographically by many miles of land and sea, but they did not sit in splendid isolation. Even though they had their own cultural distinctives, and certainly their distinctive problems, they were together. Spiritually and ecclesiastically they were one.

The New Testament provides us with three compelling examples of this unity at work.

♦ 1. Relief of the poor

An unmistakable feature of early church life was a commendable liberality in distributing material help to the poor. This was a duty enjoined on the early churches, and on us, by the apostles. Paul drew on the words of the Lord Jesus Christ Himself to enforce the point: 'I have shewed you all things, how that so labouring ye ought to support the weak, and to remember the words of the Lord Jesus, how he said, It is more blessed to give than to receive' (Acts 20:35; cf. I Cor. 16:1-4).

The early church took up its responsibility with spontaneous enthusiasm and sacrifice. The needy believers in Jerusalem and the pilgrims who had journeyed from afar at Pentecost found that their every need was met. 'All that believed were together, and had all things common; and sold their possessions and goods, and parted them to all men, as every man had need' (Acts 2:44-45).

This passage is often misrepresented as teaching that the believers sold and pooled all their possessions in order to live in some kind of communal arrangement, but there is nothing to indicate that that was the case. The selling and sharing was a continual activity. At no time did the believers reach the point at which they had sold everything they owned. Acts 2 simply tells us that they were selling their possessions and sharing the proceeds with those whom they knew to be in need, as those needs arose. They most certainly kept their houses because we read that they were 'breaking bread from house to house' (v. 46).

This generosity of spirit was not confined to immediate neighbourhoods. Almsgiving extended to meeting the needs of those at a distance. In Acts 11 we find the disciples at Antioch sending relief, every man according to his ability, 'unto the brethren which dwelt in Judea' (vs. 29,30).

Paul encouraged the believers in Corinth, and by implication throughout Achaia, to give generously in supplying the needs of the saints in Macedonia so that 'your abundance may be a supply for their want, that their abundance also may be a supply for your want: that there may be equality' (II Cor. 8:14).

The Macedonian believers themselves were noted for their own liberality, despite afflictions and 'deep poverty' (II Cor. 8:2,4). Macedonia covered an area roughly equivalent to the northern half of modern Greece, and we know of at least three churches within its borders: at Thessalonica, Philippi and Berea. The Thessalonian church is especially commended by Paul for its love of the brethren 'in all Macedonia'. He urges them, 'but we beseech you, brethren, that ye increase more and more' (I Thess. 4:9,10).

The churches of Macedonia apparently collected their alms, pooled them, and entrusted them to the apostle Paul, asking him to distribute them while on his travels. Paul described this happy task as taking upon himself 'the fellowship of the ministering of the saints' (II Cor. 8:4).

On another occasion Paul went to Jerusalem solely with the intention of distributing alms: 'But now I go unto Jerusalem to minister unto the saints. For it hath pleased them of Macedonia and Achaia to make a certain contribution for the poor saints which are at Jerusalem' (Rom. 15:25,26). From this passage we learn that *all* the churches in

Greece were involved together in helping the saints at Jerusalem.

In order that he remain above reproach, Paul entrusted the gifts collected in Macedonia to three men, and it is instructive to note, in no fewer than three verses, how these men are described. Firstly, we are told in II Cor. 8:18,19, 'And we have sent with [Titus] the brother, whose praise is in the gospel throughout all the churches; And not that only, but who was *chosen of the churches* to travel with us with this grace.' Secondly, we read that these men were '*the messengers of the churches*, and the glory of Christ' (v. 23). Finally, the Corinthians were to receive them with affection, proving to them 'and *before the churches*', i.e., those churches who had sent them, that the apostle's testimony concerning their love had been true (v. 24).

The point is that these three men were not sent by just one independent church, nor yet by three churches acting independently of each other and sending one each, but by '*the churches*' working together. There was evidently a procedure in place whereby the churches could cooperate in choosing and commissioning the right men for the task. It has to be said that in these days of fierce independency such an operation could never be undertaken, even if it was considered desirable.

Clearly the early church took 'the daily ministration' (Acts 6:1) very seriously. It involved much time and labour, so much so that the apostles found it was distracting them from their primary task of prayer and the ministry of the Word (Acts 6:2,4). For this reason they commanded the church to choose seven men 'of honest report, full of the Holy Ghost and wisdom, whom we may appoint over this business' of caring for the widows (Acts 6:3). Seven such men were duly chosen and appointed to the work, and therein we have the origin of the office of deacon in the churches of Christ.

The office of deacon, like the office of elder, is a continuing office. Its work is a continuing work. The poor are always with us, and their needs today are to be met by the dispensing of alms just as they were in the churches' earliest times. That is the deacon's work, together with the visitation of the sick and widows, bringing relief in the form of material help and words of consolation and cheer from the Scriptures. In Britain today the office of deacon has degenerated into little more than that of a caretaker who maintains the material fabric of church buildings. Does it ever occur to the modern deacon that his earliest counterparts did not have any church buildings to maintain? What did they do? They cared for the material needs of the *church*. That is a crucial distinction but one that is lost today.

The current neglect of the deacon's true work is a serious matter, and that for three reasons. In the first place, the ingathering and distribution of alms is the very purpose for which the office of deacon was created. It is the deacon's *raison d'être* and not to carry it out is to disobey the church's Head. In the second place, the consequences for both the material and spiritual well-being of the poor in our churches are dire. The priestly mercies of Christ are being denied them. In the third place, and this is the salient point, the churches are deprived of one of the most important and certainly the most expressive and tangible signs of their unity. Within the body of Christ there are materially prosperous churches and there are materially deprived churches. When we have the example of the early churches to follow and the means, in the office of deacon, to fulfil it, what grounds do we have to neglect the poor just because they are not in our own local church? It is the calling of prosperous churches to collect alms and, through the deacons, dispense them to those in need wherever that need may arise.

But there are further examples in the New Testament of unity at work.

✦ 2. Labouring together in the gospel

Our second example can be found sprinkled liberally throughout the epistles, in the expressions of endearment used by the writers towards their fellow believers. There was a deep bond of love and affection between them, no matter how far apart they happened to be geographically. Paul begins his letter to Philemon in this way, writing from Rome to Colosse: 'Paul, a prisoner of Jesus Christ, and Timothy our brother, unto Philemon our dearly beloved, and fellowlabourer, And to our beloved Apphia, and Archippus our fellowsoldier.' The same short letter ends: 'There salute thee Epaphras, my fellowprisoner in Christ Jesus; Marcus, Aristarchus, Demas, Lucas, my fellowlabourers' (Philm. 1, 2, 23, 24).

The salutations with which Paul closes his Roman, Colossian and first Corinthian letters give the same clear demonstration of the spiritual unity that bound the saints and churches together. It was a unity that expressed itself in love and mutual support among fellow labourers in the work of the gospel. They were all in it together.

Paul often used the term 'fellow' to describe his partners in the gospel. Titus was his 'fellowhelper' (II Cor. 8:23); Timothy, in addition to those quoted above from Philemon's letter, was Paul's 'fellowlabourer' (I Thess. 3:2); Epaphroditus and Archippus were his 'fellowsoldiers' (Phil. 2:25; Philm. 2); Epaphras and Tychicus were 'fellowservants' (Col. 1:7; 4:7), and in Colossians 4 Paul lists several 'fellowworkers unto the kingdom of God' (v. 4). The work of the gospel was one work, and they were all fellows together in that work. They were not working independently of each other.

This is wholly appropriate for an organism. Churches and their members are to live, think, and work together as one, one body, the body of Christ, with one heart and one soul. They are to encourage one another, love one another, care for one another, and strive together as fellow labourers in the work of the gospel.

The reality and intensity of unity amongst the New Testament churches is clearly evident from Paul's letters, by which they sent their united salutations around the world. Hence we read in the letter to Corinth, 'The churches of Asia salute you' (I Cor. 16:19), and in Paul's letter to Rome, a general greeting from all the churches together: 'The churches of Christ salute you' (Rom. 16:16). There was a close 'family relationship' between the churches, which generated mutual love, an awareness of each other's needs, and a determination to help.

Not only letters, but believers too were sent and commended from one church to another. Phebe, for example, went with Paul's commendation from the church at Cenchrea to that at Rome (Rom. 16:1,2). When the apostle commended Priscilla and Aquila, his 'helpers in Christ Jesus', to the church at Rome, he expressed not only his own personal gratitude to them for having 'laid down their own necks' for his life, but the thanks of *'all the churches* of the Gentiles' (Rom. 16:3,4).

Can one seriously imagine such greetings and commendations as these being sent today, even from the churches of one English county to those of another? In Independency the lines of such communications are broken.

Sometimes, however, questions arose in the churches. Invariably these questions concerned not just one church, nor even a number of churches, but all of them. Our third example of unity in operation is concerned with how the churches dealt with that kind of problem.

+ **3. The Jerusalem council**
When difficulties arose at Antioch over the place of circumcision in the new dispensation, it was clear that the issue at stake was not just a local one. It affected all the churches and therefore needed to be dealt with at a broader level than the local congregation. Thus we read in Acts 15 that the Antioch brethren 'determined that Paul and Barnabas, and certain other of them, should go up to Jerusalem unto the apostles and elders about the question' (Acts 15:1ff.). True, these were apostolic days and therefore very different from our own, but the point is that in seeking apostolic authority the church at Antioch did not act alone. The brethren met with the elders at Jerusalem and a church council was convened. They 'assembled with one accord' and all the problems were openly discussed.

At the close of their deliberations emissaries and letters were sent to Antioch, Syria, and Cilicia to convey to the churches in those places the authoritative conclusion of the council. As Paul and Silas travelled 'they delivered them the decrees for to keep, that were ordained of the apostles and elders which were at Jerusalem' (Acts 16:4).

We will return to these events later, but suffice to say now that here was established a pattern for the churches to continue throughout the post-apostolic era. There would be no apostles then because the canon of Scripture would be complete. When matters of common concern arose, the elders of the churches were to meet together before the Word of God, which would be their sole authority in all matters of faith and practice. Led by the Spirit of God into the truth the churches would then continue in one mind, speaking with one voice.

From these three examples, then, we are able to see that the New Testament churches not only *believed* in the unity of the church but lived in unity and *laboured* in unity. They put their faith into practice in such a way as to make our present day Evangelical and Reformed churches look woefully and shamefully deficient.

2.

The Basis
of Biblical Church Unity

What was it, then, that held those early churches together? What was the basis of their unity? What was the glue? Well, of course, it almost goes without saying that theirs was not the artificial unity of our modern-day ecumenists who are held together by compromise. Neither was it that perfect unity for which the Lord prayed in John 17, 'that they may be one, even as we are one' (v. 22). For that we must wait until we reach glory (Eph. 4:13). No, what united the churches of those days was the truth: 'Therefore love the truth and peace' says the Scripture (Zech. 8:19), and therein lies the heart of the matter.

It is not a case of either/or but both/and—truth *and* peace. True peace and Biblical unity cannot be bought at the expense of truth.

We have already established that the unity of the church is no less than the unity of Christ, in whom there is no division. What the ecumenists forget, though, is that Christ also declared Himself to be 'the truth' (John 14:6). In Him there is no falsehood or deviation, for He is the pure and absolute Truth. Therefore, just as the church is in Christ united, so she is also in Christ pure and undefiled. This means in practice that as the church militant, the church in the world, seeks to express the unity of the body, she can do so only by keeping herself in the truth. Only the truth can form the basis for genuine unity and love amongst the people of God, as we learn from the example of the apostle John: 'The elder unto the wellbeloved Gaius, whom I love *in the truth*' (III John 1; cf. v. 8).

Common Belief in the Truth

The teaching that the Lord Jesus Christ imparted to His disciples throughout His ministry was truth in all its pristine glory, untainted by even the suspicion of error. His words to Pilate are the Scriptures' own confirmation of that, 'To this end was I born, and for this cause came I into the world, that I should bear witness unto the truth' (John 18:37).

That truth Christ had received from His Father in heaven: 'My doctrine is not mine, but his that sent me,' He says (John 7:16). 'I do nothing of myself; but as my Father hath taught me, I speak these things' (cf. John 8:28-32; 12:49,50; 14:10,24; 15:15). Christ is 'the faithful witness' (Rev. 1:5). Everything He said was in perfect harmony with His Father, so there was no contradiction or discrepancy between the Father and the Son. The Son added nothing of Himself, nor left anything of the Father's unsaid. He is 'the Amen, the faithful and true witness' (Rev. 3:14), speaking with a 'verily, verily', 'truly, truly.' His testimony could therefore be relied upon as being nothing short of the very truth of God.

This divine truth, this pure doctrine from heaven, was learned by the disciples at the feet of their Master, and in it they were all united. On the day of Pentecost they were 'together', they were 'with one accord' (Acts 1:14; 2:1, 44, 46). Such was the visible unity of the Lord's disciples.

This same truth the apostles then took with them and preached wherever the Spirit of God sent them. Paul, the apostle born out of due time, assured the Corinthian believers that what he had preached to them he had been taught by no less a teacher than the Lord Himself: 'For I have received of the Lord that which also I delivered unto you' (I Cor. 11:23).

Similarly, to the Galatians he wrote, 'But I certify you, brethren, that the gospel which was preached of me is not after man. For I neither received it of man, neither was I taught it, but *by the revelation of Jesus Christ*' (Gal. 1:11,12).

Each apostle received from the Lord the same body of doctrine and preached the same Gospel wherever he was sent. Whether in Athens, Rome, or Jerusalem the same Christ was presented, the same message of salvation declared, and the same doctrines expounded, without contradiction, just as the apostles themselves had been taught by the Saviour.

What did Timothy hear from the lips of Paul? He heard 'the form of sound words', to which he was to hold fast (II Tim. 1:13) and in turn preach to others. He too preached exactly the same message. Paul sent Timothy to Corinth so that his 'son in the faith' could remind the believers there 'of my ways which be in Christ, as I teach everywhere in every church' (I Cor. 4:17).

Notice what Paul says: 'as I teach *everywhere* in *every church.*' He did not attempt to adapt the content of his message to his various hearers: 'And so ordain I in *all* churches' (I Cor. 7:17). 'As I have given order to the churches of Galatia, *even so do ye*' (I Cor. 16:1). 'God is not the author of confusion, but of peace, as in *all churches of the saints*' (I Cor. 14:33; cf. I Thess. 2:14).

From all of this it follows that the entire early church, that first generation of new dispensation believers, was grounded in the truth, even as though they had heard it from the lips of the incarnate Truth Himself. In fact Paul explicitly tells the Ephesians that they had heard Christ. Of course, they had not seen him in the flesh nor heard Him speak; but, nevertheless, through the voice of the apostle they had heard Him. They had been taught by Him 'as the truth is in Jesus' (Eph. 4:20,21). This was because Paul had preached to them the word of truth (Eph. 2:13), which is the word of Christ (Col. 3:16).

The apostles were able to do this because, in the coming of the Holy Ghost at Pentecost, He came who would 'bring all things to your remembrance, whatsoever I have said unto you' (John 14:26). Even though the Lord was no longer with them in body, His Spirit was present, guiding them into all truth: 'Howbeit when he, the Spirit of truth, is come, he will guide you into all truth: for he shall not speak of himself; but whatsoever he shall hear, that shall he speak: and he will shew you things to come. He shall glorify me' (John 16:13,14).

Here then is the bond, the glue, that held those early believers together. They were united in the same system of truth, the faith once delivered unto them by the Lord's apostles, that apostles' doctrine in which they were to continue steadfastly (Acts 2:42; Jude 3). That was the bond. The basis of their unity was truth. It is the truth, both then and now, which binds the Lord's people together such that they are all of one mind. That is the essence of Biblical church unity: it is to share a common belief in the eternal, unchangeable truth.

Doctrinal Succession

What we must realize is that that same body of truth which united the churches of Galatia and Achaia with those of Jerusalem and Ephesus, every succeeding generation of the Lord's people have had in their possession. It was not unique to the days of the apostles. They were inspired by the Holy Spirit to write it down for us, so that we have it now in our own hands without alteration, no more and no less. Therefore the unity that they experienced in their day is no less accessible to us.

The church today has no excuse for disunity merely because she has come such a long way in time from the golden age of the apostles. We have the same faith, the same apostles' doctrine, the same word of truth as the early church possessed. This is the true apostolic succession— not a succession of office or authority but a succession of doctrine, of truth down the ages. Never has the church been without it: 'I have given them thy word,' said Christ, 'thy word is truth' (John 17:14,17).

The church in our day has received the truth as a glorious heritage. From generation to generation that heritage, like the athlete's baton, has been handed down until we are entrusted with it for safe keeping in these closing years of the twentieth century.

The consequence of this succession is that we enjoy a blessed organic unity with the saints of former days. It must be said that this is not sufficiently appreciated by us, if at all. If we are united with the saints of past generations in a common belief in the truth, being guided by the same Spirit of truth, that is a great blessing and we can live, or should live, in the consciousness of it. We should live in conscious fellowship with the church of the past. No individual believer, no local church or denomination of churches can sit in historical isolation, any more than it can in geographical isolation, because all are members together of the same body.

Maybe one of the reasons why this consciousness has been lost is the church's ignorance of her history, but I believe there is another even more important reason. We live today in an age of unashamed individualism. The 'rights' and desires of the individual are considered paramount. He is independent. He is responsible only to and for himself. He sets his own goals and ethical standards in isolation from all that has gone before, and even to the disregard of others around him. He goes his own way and seeks his own ends for his own personal fulfilment.

Independence is the spirit of the age. Wives seek independence from their husbands. Husbands want independence from their wives. Parents want to be independent from their interfering children, and when the children grow up they want to be independent from their aged, burdensome parents. The results of this in society are clear to see as abortion, child abuse, neglect of the elderly, and other social evils abound.

Needless to say, such individualism has no place in the church of Jesus Christ. Following the example of our Saviour, who 'pleased not himself ', 'we then that are strong ought to bear the infirmities of the weak, and not to please ourselves' (Rom. 15:1-3; cf. I Cor. 8:13; Gal. 6:2; Heb. 10:24). Each member of the body, each living stone in the building, occupies a position in relation to all the others, irrespective of time and place. We hold the truth in relation to both those who have gone before and to those who will come after us.

This is a principle brought out clearly in Paul's letters to Timothy. Paul writes that he had received the gospel, the 'glorious gospel' he calls it, as a sacred trust (I Tim. 1:11). It was committed to him for safe keeping. He in turn passed it on to Timothy with the command that he was to hold on to it: '*hold fast* the form of sound words, which thou hast heard of me, in faith and love which is in Christ Jesus. That good thing which was committed unto thee *keep* by the Holy Ghost which dwelleth in us' (II Tim. 1:13,14).

Likewise Timothy was to pass on the baton of truth to the generation after him: 'And the things that thou hast heard of me among many witnesses, the same commit thou to faithful men'. And what were those faithful men to do in their turn but 'to teach others also' (II Tim. 2:2).

In a similar vein, Paul writes to the brethren at Thessalonica, this time using the term 'tradition' to emphasize the continuity of truth: 'stand fast, and hold the traditions which ye have been taught, whether by word, or our epistle' (II Thess. 2:15).

That which our fathers have taught us we in turn are to pass on to our children, for they are the church of their generation. We have a responsibility to them, 'shewing to the generation to come the praises of the LORD, and his strength, and his wonderful works that he hath done.... That the generation to come might know them, even the children which should be born; who should arise and declare them to their children: that they might set their hope in God, and not forget the works of God, but keep his commandments' (Ps. 78:4-7). In this way each child of God, from Adam to the last elect soul, is related to and united with every other.

We are to 'hold the traditions'. We are to hold fast to the apostles' doctrine that has been passed down to us, the Word of God, for that is the bond that unites *us*, just as it united the churches of two thousand years ago. It unites the churches both among themselves and with the church of past and future generations.

There is a continuity of doctrine, originating in heaven, woven into the very fabric of church history as an unbroken thread. Ever present, it unites the whole church until the gathering of the elect is complete, for 'the Son of God, from the beginning to the end of the world, gathers, defends, and preserves to Himself by His Spirit and Word, out of the whole human race, a church *agreeing in true faith*'.[1]

Truth Divides?

The objection is often made, however, that rather than unite, truth divides, doctrine divides. There is certainly a sense in which that is so. Truth does divide—it divides from the lie. The churches of the New Testament were not only to unite in the truth but also to shun those who were in error: 'mark them which cause divisions and offences contrary to the doctrine which ye have learned; and avoid them' (Rom. 16:17). He who preaches 'another gospel', 'let him be accursed' (Gal. 1:6-9).

To the Thessalonians Paul issues a strong and what may appear to us a most unloving command, 'in the name of our Lord Jesus Christ, that ye withdraw yourselves from every brother that walketh disorderly, and not after the tradition which ye received of us' (II Thess. 3:6). This is what marks out true unity from the false unity of the ecumenical movement. When the truth is rejected, the lie must be withstood and shunned.

1　*Heidelberg Catechism*. Lord's Day 21, Q./.A. 54.

The cause of disunity is always error, never truth. In Philippians 3:2 Paul writes, 'beware of the concision.' He is warning the church of certain Judaizers, 'evil workers' he calls them, who were insisting that the rite of circumcision should still be performed, even on Christian converts. They were putting value on the outward rite, while denying the inner reality of heart circumcision (cf. Rom. 2:28,29). By a play on words the Holy Spirit underlines the very point we are making here. By their erroneous insistence on the cutting of the flesh (*circum*cision), they were guilty of the mutilation (*con*cision) of the body of Christ. They were making a cut in the church, causing a tear and division, rending the church apart (cf. Rom. 16:17,18).

The approach of the liberal and the ecumenist is to say that the church is *in search of* the truth and that different parts of the body find it in different expressions. They then go on to argue that each such 'expression of truth' is equally legitimate and therefore must be respected by all. That road leads only to the blind alley of relativism, where there is no truth and no error, where everyone has the right to believe what he wants to believe.

No, the church is not in search of the truth, she *has* the truth (cf. I Tim. 3:15). She is the custodian of the truth. She has the Word of God and she has the Spirit of truth as her Interpreter.

The church has indeed come a long way in time from the age of the apostles. Two thousand years is plenty of time to account for the multitude of heresies, lies, and half-truths that plague the churches today. A tendency to depart from the truth was evident very early in church history, so much so that it surprised even the apostle Paul (cf. Gal. 1:6). It was present even within the apostolic band (cf. Gal. 2:11), and subsequent history is littered with departures from the faith, prompting what is the only Biblical response from those who remain faithful: separation for the re-forming of the church anew. 'Wherefore come out from among them, and be ye separate, saith the Lord' (II Cor. 6:17). That is the Biblical pattern, of which the sixteenth century Reformation is such a shining example.

Yes, truth divides from those who oppose it, but it unites in a most beautiful way, crossing geographical and historical barriers, all who love it and who walk in its ways. In the church of Jesus Christ no one holds the truth in isolation.

3.

The Expression
of Biblical Church Unity

To summarize thus far, we have sought to establish that the basis for church unity is belief in the truth. We have noticed that this was the bond holding together the churches of the New Testament. They were united in a common belief in the truth of God as it had been delivered to them by the apostles.

We have noticed also that the truth is no less than Christ Himself, for He said, 'I am... the truth' (John 14:6). To believe in the truth is no less than to believe in Christ. That is faith. We can say, therefore, that the bond uniting believers and churches is 'the faith'. 'There is one body,... one faith' (Eph. 4:4-6). Objectively, 'the faith' is that body of truth contained in the Scriptures, it is that 'faith which was once delivered unto the saints' (Jude 3), while subjectively it is that which unites us to Christ. Understood in both senses, faith is God's precious gift to us by His grace. We believe 'according to the working of his mighty power' (Eph. 1:19; cf. Col. 1:29 and Eph. 2:8-9).

The question we consider now is how this gift of God expresses itself. Does faith stay silent? Does faith not speak? Scripture provides us with the emphatic answer that, yes, faith does speak. It must and it will speak.

Confession of Faith

Faith cannot remain silent: 'I believed, therefore have I spoken' confessed the psalmist (Ps. 116:10). Faith has a voice that even all the enmity and persecutions of the world cannot put to silence: 'We having the same spirit of faith, according as it is written, I believed, and therefore have I spoken; we also believe, and therefore speak' (II Cor. 4:13).

It is out of the abundance of the heart that the mouth speaks (Matt. 12:34). The mouth provides the evidence by which we know the spiritual state of the heart, whether it is good or corrupt. If a man has evil treasure in his heart he will bring forth evil things from his mouth, but 'a good man out of the good treasure of the heart bringeth forth good things' (Matt. 12:35).

Where there is faith, a heart indwelt by the Spirit of truth, there will be a mouth speaking wisdom, making known the faithfulness of God to all generations (Ps. 49:3; 89:1). Where the Lord God is sanctified in the heart there will be a tongue ever ready to give an answer to every man that asks a reason of the hope that is in him (I Pet. 3:15).

Scripture calls this speech of faith the *confession* of faith. The believer confesses his faith before men. That truth which we believe we also confess. The Bible constantly maintains a vital link between the heart and the mouth, between faith and the confession of faith. It goes even so far as to identify that confession with salvation itself, for where there is confession of Christ, there must of necessity be faith in the heart. The two cannot be divorced: 'If thou shalt confess with thy mouth the Lord Jesus, and shalt believe in thine heart that God hath raised him from the dead, thou shalt be saved. For with the heart man believeth unto righteousness; and with the mouth confession is made unto salvation' (Rom. 10:9-10).

Credo

It is possible to distinguish three levels at which this confession of faith is made.

1. First of all, as should be clear from the Scriptures we have already referred to, confession is made at a personal level. We all as individual believers confess our faith before men. We testify of the truth that is in us, of that which we believe.

Scripture has given us the confession of Peter, 'Thou art the Christ, the Son of the living God' (Matt. 16:16); of Martha, 'Yea, Lord: I believe that thou art the Christ, the Son of God, which should come into the world' (John 11:27); and of the Ethiopian eunuch, 'I believe that Jesus Christ is the Son of God' (Acts 8:37).

But confession does not end there. It is not confined to the individual. Even Peter's confession can be understood as being the united confession of the disciples, Peter so often acting as their spokesman.

This brings us to the second level at which confession is made: the local church.

2. A gathered company of the Lord's people, being of one mind, confess together 'we believe'. It was Paul's prayer for the church at Rome that they might 'with one mind and *one mouth* glorify God, even the father of our Lord Jesus Christ' (Rom. 15:6). In this manner each church becomes a light set upon a hill, a beacon shining out into this dark, sin-benighted world. With every member speaking the same thing, she is like a trumpet giving out a sure and certain sound, telling forth the truth of her God.

Now there are some Christians for whom the whole idea of a church creed or confession of faith is anathema. 'No creed but Christ' is their catchy motto. Since this attitude stems from a fundamental misunderstanding of the nature and character of a creed, we will digress to explain this in greater detail.

For a Biblical description of a creed we need look no further than to Luke 1:1. A creed is 'a declaration of those things which are most surely believed among us'. It is important that we recognize a creed as having two aspects, both of which can be identified in this text.

Firstly, it is a declaration. That is clearly understood. A creed is an objective statement declaring what a church believes to be true concerning God. It forms an answer to the question 'What is truth?' It is easy for us to assert that we believe the truth, but it is also very glib. It does not say anything. There is not a church on the face of the earth, however apostate it has become, that will not say it believes the truth. The important thing is to state what we understand the truth to be, what we understand the Bible to say. That is what a creed or confession of faith does. It thereby serves as a standard by which a local church is identified and around which its members unite in opposition to error and the world.

But if we leave our definition of creed there, I believe we will have missed the most important aspect, indeed the whole point of what is meant by 'confession of faith'. A creed is something far more than just an objective standard. There is a prominent subjective element. This is evident from the expression 'most surely believed', as found in Luke 1:1. A creed ought not to be considered merely as a collection of doctrinal statements to which believers give their mental assent, even assuming it is Scripturally sound. That may well satisfy an enquirer as to a church's orthodoxy, but in itself it is not enough. Ephesus was strictly orthodox, yet there was something of the utmost importance that she was lacking: her first love (cf. Rev. 2:1-7). She had lost her *zeal* for the Lord and His truth.

Confession of faith is not a cold, clinical assent to a set of doctrines. There is something far deeper and more spiritual involved. Real confession arises from the heart. It is living and vibrant. It is not just an intellectual activity but is also a matter of the heart and of the soul. It carries conviction and warmth as the living testimony of the church. In her corporate confession of faith a church is affirming with all her heart, mind and soul, '*WE BELIEVE....*'

A creed is not like a political manifesto that someone draws up and calls on others to endorse. A creed is the voice of a church's united faith. It is not something brought in from outside, but originates in the hearts of the members themselves—hearts indwelt by the Holy Spirit of truth. It has been well said that 'the true use of a creed is not to set forth what men must believe, but to record what men do believe' (W H P Faunce).

Confession is the work of the Spirit. That document of objective doctrinal statements which many so decry is a fruit of the Holy Spirit, a work of faith, a spontaneous outpouring from the heart. It is the common confession of a company of the Lord's people gathered together by Christ into a local church. It is therefore to be maintained, outworked, and cherished by that church as a most precious gift from her heavenly Father. When a church is thus united in the faith, giving expression to her unity by common confession, that is truly wonderful and cause for thanksgiving to God.

But we must go further because, wonderful though that may be, it still does not give full expression to the unity of Christ's body. There is a broader unity, as we have seen, and that too is to be outworked in the life and confession of the churches.

3. When a number of churches, perhaps scattered over large

distances as were those of the apostolic age, confess together the same confession, speak the same thing, being united together in the truth also with the church of past generations, that is more wonderful still. That is a more complete reflection of the unity of the body of Christ on earth. That is the unity of the Spirit. In other words, it is Biblical church unity.

Paul besought the church at Corinth, together with 'all that in every place call upon the name of Jesus Christ our Lord' to 'all speak the same thing' (I Cor. 1:2,10). The idea of confession therefore extends beyond the local situation. Churches and saints covering large geographical areas who are united in the truth are required to make common confession of that truth. It is their calling to speak the same thing and not to contradict one another, causing confusion and misunderstanding and thereby bringing dishonour to the name of the Lord.

Clearly enunciating what they believe the truth of the Word of God to be, churches are called to unite in common confession of their faith. They are to identify with that confession, defend it against the attacks and slanders of the world, oppose on its basis all errors and heresies, and give all the glory to the God and Father of our Lord Jesus Christ.

It is true that occasionally during the twentieth century this responsibility has been recognized to a degree. Some churches have sincerely sought to express a broader unity by the forging of stronger ties between themselves. Invariably, however, these attempts have been on the basis of wholly inadequate 'statements of faith'. Presbyterianism too, if it is not applied Biblically, can give the appearance of being little more than an accommodation of Independency under a broad 'presbyterian' umbrella.

The point of Presbyterian and Reformed church government is not that it can accommodate heterodoxy. No, the point and the beauty of Presbyterian and Reformed church government is that it unites churches of a common confession. This means in practice that a believer can travel from one side of the world to another and find a unity—a uniformity even—in church doctrine and practice. Wherever he may be he will find a spiritual home from home. He will find churches of one mind speaking the same things.

It is not without significance that the creedal standards of the continental Reformed churches (the Heidelberg Catechism, the Belgic Confession and the Canons of Dordrecht) are together called 'the three forms of *unity*'.

The Historic Creeds

Again the importance of the historic aspect to all of this needs emphasizing. Since Biblical church unity embraces the saints of every generation, we need to express that historic unity by joining in common confession with our fathers.

The creeds and confessions that our fathers have handed down to us, right from the early days of the New Testament church, are not just interesting historical documents of no practical use or relevance, even though that seems to be the prevailing view today. The fact that they are largely forgotten, ignored or even disparaged in our day says a great deal about the spiritual condition of the churches and their leaders. It is a sign of the times in which we live that men will not endure sound doctrine, and the creeds are full of sound doctrine. On the one hand the ecumenical spirit of compromise has displaced all zeal for dogmatic theology. On the other hand a mystic subjectivism, seen in its most advanced form in the charismatic movement, but present in principle in many more orthodox circles, has undermined the churches' hold on the Scriptures as the truth, the final and complete revelation of God to His people. These twin scourges leave no place for the creeds.

But even among those who acknowledge the historic creeds and confessions as being of some value, it must be said that they are given only lip-service. By ministers they are considered as little more than useful doctrinal handbooks and reference tools to help in sermon preparation. Perhaps on the occasion of an anniversary they are taken off the shelf and dusted, so to speak, but to the congregation they mean little and remain unread.

No one would deny that the confessions are useful aids to Bible study, but to see this as being their only rôle today is to miss their real significance. They have long ceased to be what they should be: a living confession rising from the hearts of the Lord's people united down through history such that they affirm with one voice, 'we most surely believe.'

It has to be said that, in their understanding of the meaning and significance of the creeds, the majority of churches today, and we are talking now about conservative Evangelical churches, have missed the point by a mile. They have failed to see them for what they really are. The creeds are not text books. They are living confessions of living faith. Combine this failure with an ignorance of and indifference to the church's historic unity, and the loss of visible unity becomes inevitable, since it is through the creeds that it is expressed.

Many if not all of the creeds and confessions were formulated in the heat of intense theological controversy. They were the church's response to heresy, born out of a love and concern for the truth and a need to define and defend it. The saints raised up their creeds as mighty bulwarks against the enemies of truth. It was the heresy of Arianism that gave rise to the Nicene Creed in AD 325. The other trinitarian creeds, the Athanasian and the Chalcedonian, again were written in response to errors concerning the person of our Lord Jesus Christ. But it was the Reformation that produced the fullest expressions of revealed theology. From that work of God, by which He delivered His church from the evil darkness of medieval popery, came such clear and systematic declarations of Christian doctrine as remain unsurpassed to this day among uninspired writings.

These points in history mark giant steps forward in the church's understanding of the truth. But we must ask ourselves, how did the church arrive at such clearer understanding of truth? Was it not by the Holy Spirit Himself? 'When he, the Spirit of Truth, is come, he will guide you into all truth' (John 16:13). The creeds are the product of the Holy Spirit living and working in the hearts and minds of God's people, causing them, often under severe physical hardship, to see the truth with a clarity and declare it with a sharpness hitherto not known or heard. The calling of the church today is to take hold of that truth into which her fathers were guided, and confess it with them.

Does the faith of the children differ from the faith of their fathers? God forbid if that should be so! Has truth changed? It is not for each generation to discover the truth for itself, as the liberal and the modernist would have us to believe, but to receive it with thanksgiving from the hands of those who have gone before, and confess it before men.

This does not rule out development in our understanding of truth, and continuing reformation down the ages. As the Spirit builds on what has gone before, the church grows in her knowledge of the truth. But the truth itself does not change, even as Christ does not change. He is 'Jesus Christ the same yesterday, and today, and for ever' (Heb. 13:8), and His infallible, unchangeable Word is always to be our supreme authority.

Against those churches that take their confessional standards seriously, the charge is sometimes made that they give them an authority equal to that of Holy Scripture. There are two comments to be made in reply. In the first place, it is doubtful whether the charge is ever actually true, but, in the second place, even if it were a valid charge, the objection is misdirected, since the fault lies not with the confession, but with the individual, church, or denomination giving it the undue authority.

The authority of a creed is a *derived* authority and is therefore always subordinate to that of Scripture. The creeds are not infallible, so with a clearer understanding of Scripture it is right and in order for churches to amend them accordingly.

There is a parallel here with the situation we find in the opening verses of Luke's gospel. The confessions are like those declarations to which Luke refers, setting in order 'those things which are most surely believed among us'. They are subordinate to that written by those, like Luke himself, having 'perfect understanding of all things from the very first'. As at all times when we read or hear the words of uninspired men, we must search the Scriptures, so that we might 'know the certainty of those things, wherein thou hast been instructed' (Luke 1:1-4; cf. Acts 17:10,11).

But the danger today, in these times of doctrinal laxity, lies not so much in giving the confessions too much authority, as not enough. Once a church or denomination becomes embarrassed by its stated confession and quietly leaves it to gather dust on the shelf, or allows diversity of opinion on matters that are judged to be unconcerned with 'the substance of the faith', then the enemy is at the door, if not already rampaging through the house. The churches no longer speak with one voice, and divisions, with all the disruption and pain they incur, inevitably follow.

By subscribing to the great definitions of truth from former days the church maintains the vital link with the church of her fathers. She stands with them and expresses her organic unity with them, and thereby the church of the present experiences conscious fellowship with the church of the past.

Doctrinal independence from the church of the past is the hallmark of sectarianism. Sects, by their very nature, reject and despise the creeds and confessions. They thrive in a climate of theological individualism. They epitomize the idea of all men believing that which is right in their own eyes and then drawing others after them. In contrast, churches that 'hold the traditions' will with gladness in their hearts join their fathers in common confession of the truth which they all as one believe.

If church unity is to be Biblical, therefore, the churches must be *confessional* churches.

4.

The Keeping
of Biblical Church Unity

I. The Common Teaching

When the Bible speaks of our calling with regard to church unity it never speaks of *creating* unity or of *becoming* united. This is because unity already exists as a principle intrinsic to the body of Christ. The idea of Christ's church being divided and having to 'come together' is something quite foreign to Scripture. Our calling is rather to 'walk worthy of the vocation wherewith ye are called... endeavouring to *keep* the unity of the Spirit in the bond of peace. There is one body and one spirit, even as ye are called in one hope of your calling; one Lord, one faith, one baptism, one God and Father of all, who is above all, and through all, and in you all' (Eph. 1:1; 4:1-6).

The calling of churches, therefore, is not to manufacture the unity of the Spirit but to keep it, to maintain it.

But that does not mean we may be passive. Keeping the unity of the Spirit involves effort. The natural inclination of our hearts is toward error, self-seeking, and pride. It is so easy to let the truth slip, to wander from the central path and thus break the bond of unity. For this reason unity has to be worked at. We can be so independent by nature, deceiving ourselves that we can go it alone; but there is no place for independence in the body of Christ. We are all related one to another as members of the same body and called to strive together for the cause of the unity of that body.

The Philippians were to 'stand fast in one spirit, with one mind *striving together* for the faith of the gospel' (Phil. 1:27). So must we in our day strive together with one mind, earnestly contending for the faith once delivered (Jude 3). There is work involved. There are battles to be fought: battles against the flesh, the devil, and the encroachment of heresy and worldly thought into the church.

Notice, in the first place, the verbs the apostles use: 'endeavour' (Eph. 4:1), 'strive' (Phil. 1:27) and 'earnestly contend' (Jude 3). These expressions indicate activity and convey to us the difficulty of the task, the toil, the sweat and tears, the spiritual graft entailed. It is not something that comes to us naturally or without effort, but calls for labour, as well as for grace and humility.

In the second place we should notice that it is a task performed within the context of the local church. It is in the local church that the body of Christ, with whose unity we are concerned, is manifest. Hence, we find that at Ephesus it was not an *ad hoc* gathering of believers that was to endeavour to keep the unity of the Spirit, but a local church properly organized, and governed by ordained officers.

The significance of this becomes clear later in Ephesians 4, where Paul explains the nature of the work the church has been called to do. He tells us *how* she keeps the unity of the Spirit:

> 'And he gave some, apostles; and some, prophets; and some, evangelists; and some, pastors and teachers; For the perfecting of the saints, for the work of the ministry, for the edifying of the body of Christ: Till we all come in the unity of the faith, and of the knowledge of the Son of God, unto a perfect man, unto the measure of the stature of the fulness of Christ: That we henceforth be no more children, tossed to and fro, and carried about with every wind of doctrine, by the sleight of men, and cunning craftiness, whereby they lie in wait to deceive; But speaking the truth in love, may grow up into him in all things, which is the head, even Christ: From whom the whole body fitly joined together and compacted by that which every joint supplieth, according to the effectual working in the measure of every part, maketh increase of the body unto the edifying of itself in love' (Eph. 4:11-16).

This passage explains to us the principle means by which the church maintains the unity of the body: it is by the preaching of the Word. Since this preaching is to be found only in the local church, the child of God must become a *member* of a local church, as we shall now see.

Church Membership

The importance of church membership cannot be overstated. Christ gathers His people into local, organized, instituted congregations in the midst of whom He dwells. Private worship in the secret place, family worship, and listening to tape-recorded sermons all have their appropriate place in the believer's life. They are all, to varying degrees, beneficial to his spiritual well-being, but none of them may be considered a substitute for church membership and attendance at the means of grace, chief of which is the preaching of the Word. None of them may be considered a substitute for the corporate worship of God and the experience of the communion of saints, confessing together the one faith. This is because in church membership a principle is at work.

The world has a saying that 'no man is an island'. This idea surely finds its highest expression in the church of Jesus Christ. Christians are not independent: they are interrelated and interdependent as members together of the one body of Christ. When a believer joins a local church he is giving expression to his membership of that body, i.e., that he is a Christian. A believer who wilfully remains outside of the local church is a paradox. He is saying, in effect, 'I am a member of the body of Christ, but not a member.' Such a one will find no support in Scripture for his position.

The seriousness of this case becomes clear when we consider the position of someone who leaves the local church. In withdrawing from the local manifestation of Christ's body he is indicating to all around him that he is not a member of the body, i.e., not a believer. Indeed, that is the principle underlying the final step in church discipline, excommunication. A member who refuses to repent shows all the signs that he does not belong to Christ's body, hence he may no longer continue as a member of its local manifestation.

No Christian has the right or authority to voluntarily withdraw and absent himself from the local church and maintain an independent existence. He is duty bound as a member of the body to join himself to the local church. 'And let us consider one another to provoke unto love and to good works: Not forsaking the assembling of ourselves together, as the manner of some is' (Heb. 10:24,25).

Anyone is free to 'attend church', but a believer will seek to follow the example of Saul of Tarsus who, not long after his conversion, 'assayed to *join himself* to the disciples' at Jerusalem (Acts 9:26). The word 'join' here indicates that he did not wish simply to *attend* the disciples' meetings, but to cement or glue himself to their number, and be one with them in a corporate body. This was in contrast to a number of people in Jerusalem who had earlier refused to join, or cement, themselves to the disciples (Acts 5:13).

As the structure of the New Testament local church took shape, church offices were instituted. Pastors, elders and deacons were ordained to fulfil, in the name of Christ, the teaching, ruling and priestly functions in the church. The Scriptures teach us that it is the Lord's will for His people to acknowledge these officers, honour them and submit to them: 'We beseech you, brethren, to know them which labour among you, and are over you in the Lord, and admonish you, and esteem them very highly in love for their work's sake' (I Thess. 5:12,13). 'Let the elders that rule well be counted worthy of double honour, especially they who labour in the word and doctrine' (I Tim. 5:17). 'Obey them that have the rule over you, and submit yourselves: for they watch over your souls, as they that must give account...' (Heb. 13:17). All these are the responsibilities of *membership*. Mere attendance is not enough.

A believer must search out and join himself to the purest manifestation of the church that he can find in his neighbourhood, a local church that keeps herself united on the line of truth, one in mind and confession. It is only as a member of such a local church, that a Christian can even begin to experience and appreciate the unity of the body of Christ.

The most important reason for this is the necessity of preaching, and only in the local church will the believer find preaching.

The 'Chief Sinew'

At this point we must stop to ask ourselves the question, What is preaching? Or to put it slightly differently, What constitutes a preacher? Perhaps the relevance of this is not immediately apparent, but hopefully will become so as we progress.

Briefly, the Scriptures teach us that a preacher is a man through whom Christ Himself is pleased to speak and be heard. In Romans 10: 14 the apostle writes, 'How then shall they call on him in whom they have not believed? and how shall they believe in him [of][1] *whom they have not heard?* and how shall they hear without a preacher?' A preacher does not speak in his own private capacity but as the mouthpiece of Christ, so that it is *His* voice that is heard in the preaching. We have already mentioned this in relation to the Ephesians, whom Paul says had, through his preaching, heard and been taught by Christ (Eph. 4:20-21). It is Christ, no less, who speaks, calls, instructs, and builds up His church through the preacher, as the apostle is telling us in II Corinthians 5:20: 'Now then we are ambassadors for Christ, *as though God did beseech you by us*: we pray you *in Christ's stead,* be ye reconciled to God'. The Lord says to His preachers, 'He that heareth you, heareth me' (Luke 10:16).

Calvin understood this perfectly, saying that Christ 'uses the ministry of men to declare openly his will to us by mouth, as a sort of delegated work, not by transferring to them his right and honour, but only that through their mouths *he may do his own work*—just as a workman uses a tool to do his work'.[2]

This being so, it should be evident that Christ does not speak through every believer, giving all the right to preach, but only through those whom He calls, ordains, and sends to be His ambassadors or heralds. As the apostle said, 'And how shall they preach, except they be *sent?*' (Rom. 10:14). The unavoidable implication is that without this sending forth it is impossible for a man to preach, however naturally gifted he may be (cf. Jer. 23:21).

There are serious shortcomings in the popular understanding of preaching. It is usually understood that if a man (or even woman these days) has a reasonable knowledge of the Scriptures and of Christian doctrine, and some competence in public speaking, then he has all that is required to make him a preacher. But that is not what we learn from the Scriptures. Even if a man has a strong desire and heart-felt conviction that he is called to preach, that is still not enough.

When Christ sends forth a man to preach He never does so

---

1 The preposition *of* is not present in the Greek.

2 John Calvin. *Institutes of the Christian Religion.* The Westminster Press, 1960; 2:1053.

independently of the *church*. The *church* is the pillar and ground of the truth, and it is to her that the task of preaching the gospel has been given, being a part of her great commission (Matt. 28:19-20). She fulfils this task through those whom she calls to serve as minister in the local church, setting them apart by the 'laying on of the hands of the presbytery', as in the case of Timothy (I Tim. 4:14; see also Acts 13:1-3). Only one who is called in this way by the church, has any rightful claim to be a preacher, and to be heard as one sent by Christ.

Moreover, it is important to understand that when Christ calls a man to preach He calls him to *office*, the preaching office of the church. The separation of the activity of preaching from the office of preaching has led to many unbiblical practices over the years, such as lay preaching, and itinerant evangelism. In Ephesians 4:11 the apostle lists *offices*—some temporary, such as apostle, and prophet, but also the continuing office of pastor and teacher. It is striking, and sobering to reflect on the fact, that the New Testament provides us with no instance of preaching other than by a man holding a teaching office. Indeed, anyone else would not be speaking with Christ's voice and authority, but merely as an impostor acting out the part.

But what does all this have to do with the unity of the church? We will let Calvin answer from his *Institutes*: 'nothing fosters mutual love more fittingly than for men to be bound together with this bond: one is appointed pastor to teach the rest, and those bidden to be pupils receive the common teaching from one mouth.'[3] He says again, 'this human ministry... is the chief sinew by which believers are held together in one body.'[4]

Calvin's expression 'the common teaching' is a striking one. The Lord speaks with just one voice, and when His delegated, sent ministers fulfil their calling faithfully, they too will speak with one voice so that the teaching they give will be common to all. They will speak the words of Him who sent them. When 'preachers' are merely self-appointed, free agents not having been ordained by God and set apart by the church to office, then they are not the mouthpieces of Christ, cannot speak with the authority of Christ, and undermine the unity of the church.

---

3 Ibid. p. 1054.
4 Ibid. p. 1055

Where the teaching ministry is at variance with the churches' faith and confession there can only be confusion and disruption; but where there is a common faith, confession, *and teaching*, all under the supervision of Godly elders, there is a triple cord that cannot easily be broken.

The Unity of the Spirit

Unity is the work of the Spirit of Christ, as through faithful preaching by God-appointed pastors and teachers He works to perfect the saints, to edify the body of Christ, till all come in the unity of the faith and of the knowledge of the Son of God unto a perfect man. Put simply, the unity of the church is maintained through the ministry of the Word. It is in the preaching that Christ speaks by His Spirit and continues His earthly ministry, bringing to His people the eternal Word of Truth that has been handed down to them.

That divine truth that Christ received from His Father, which He imparted to His disciples, and which they in turn preached to Gentile and Jew in the early years of the New Testament church, is taught and heard today where true preaching is practiced. And just as that truth united then, so it unites now. Just as it is the Spirit who guides us into all truth and by whom we confess that truth, so it is by the Spirit that unity is maintained in the church. The Holy Spirit is the unifying force, maintaining the purity of the gospel, ensuring that what is preached is no more and no less than 'the form of sound words' given to the apostles, and that the confession of the church today is at one with her confession down through the ages as she gives voice to the truth that is in her.

Little wonder that what we are dealing with is called 'the unity of the Spirit'. There is nothing of man in it. Not even the minister of a church can create or enforce unity amongst his flock. Unity is not forced upon believers against their stubborn, independent wills but is worked in them by the gracious, powerful ministrations of the Holy Spirit. He works in the churches to maintain and bring to expression the glorious unity of the body of Christ.

To be disunited, to be tossed to and fro, carried about with every wind of doctrine, says Paul, is to be like children, immature. That is invariably the situation one finds where there is failure or incompetence in the pulpit. That was the situation at Corinth. Unity, on the other hand, fostered by a regular faithful pulpit ministry, indicates maturity, the saints having 'grown up' into Him.

Now, quite obviously, it is no easy task for some of the Lord's people to find such a faithful local church: large tracts of the British Isles are spiritual wastelands. But still the believer is not discharged of his responsibility. This may mean that he will have to travel several miles to find a church. If that is not possible he may have to join a church that falls short in some measure. In this case it is his duty to seek the reformation of the church using all the means at his disposal within the rules of government of that church. If reformation proves impossible, then it may be practicable for a number of like-minded believers to come together and work for the establishment of a separate church.

If none of these things proves feasible then the lonely believer, while deserving our sympathy, may well question whether he should be living in such a spiritual desert.

5.

The Keeping of Biblical Church Unity

II. Biblical Ecumenism

As much as it is the calling of the individual believer to belong to a local church, is it not also the calling of local churches to manifest the broader unity of Christ's body?

It is at this point that we introduce the question of institutional or organizational church unity, and there is surely an irony in that this is probably the most contentious aspect of our subject. Where there exists amongst churches a unity of both faith and confession, ought not that spiritual, organic unity be reflected in an institutional unity?

It is our purpose to show that institutional unity is to be a feature of the churches, as a Biblical and logical consequence of all that we have said thus far. In this chapter we will confine ourselves to a few general principles before, in the final chapter, considering a specific case drawn from the New Testament.

Order

The only church institution recognized in the New Testament is the local church. We have already discovered, however, that the exhortations to unity found in the epistles reached out far beyond the confines of any one local congregation. We have noticed too that there was a day-to-day, practical unity. The early churches clearly understood that their corporate life and responsibilities did not end with the official worship services of the Lord's Day, but continued through each day of the week to become manifest in practical ways, touching the lives of fellow believers in far-away congregations. While the churches were clearly autonomous, i.e., self-governing under the rule and authority of Christ alone, they were not independent of each other.

In Chapter 1 we noted that the church is the body of Christ (Eph. 1:22,23). A body is a living, united organism, and in much the same way as a body is structured and organized, so the church in the world has structure and order: 'For as we have many members in one body, and all members have not the same office: So we, being many, are one body in Christ, and every one members one of another' (Rom. 12:4,5).

Similarly, the church is a building, 'Ye, as lively stones, are built up a spiritual house' (I Peter 2:5), and in like manner the church has order and unity.

The life of the church is to be outworked through local congregations in such a way that there exists amongst them a unity of faith and purpose, as we find in the New Testament—churches bound together by the truth for the work of the gospel. On viewing the church scene one would hope to see decency and order, not a confused ecclesiastical hotchpotch.

In some Christian circles the very idea of organization meets with abhorrence, as though there is something intrinsically super-spiritual about disorganization and disorder. But in all of His works our God is the God of order, not of confusion. This is strikingly evident in creation. We know that history too is not a haphazard sequence of chance happenings, but follows the perfect order of God's eternal decree.

Israel, the church of the Old Testament, was highly organized and structured in all aspects of her life; and when we look into the New Testament we find again that there is firm emphasis placed upon order in the churches. The church at Corinth comes in for particular attention in this regard: 'Let all things be done decently and in order' (I Cor 14:40; cf. v.33; 16:1). Paul rejoiced to see the order in the church at Colosse (Col. 2:5), while exhorting Titus to 'set in order the things that are wanting' in the churches on Crete (Titus 1:5). Similarly, the reason why the apostle gave Timothy instruction concerning elders and deacons, was 'that thou mayest know how thou oughtest to behave thyself in the house of God, which is the church of the living God, the pillar and ground of the truth' (I Tim. 3:15).

These passages were written concerning specific local congregations, but their effect was to put into place a common practice throughout the early church, thereby establishing an order that became a further expression of her unity. The church order the apostle was at pains to teach Titus, Timothy, and the Corinthians was no different from that which he rejoiced to see at Colosse. He writes, 'For this cause have I sent unto you Timotheus, who is my beloved son, and faithful in the Lord, who shall bring you into remembrance of my ways which be in Christ, *as I teach everywhere in every church*' (I Cor. 4:17; cf. 7:17; 11:16; 14:33; 16:1; II Cor. 11:28).

There was a degree of organization amongst the New Testament churches. By this we do not mean a hierarchical structure, far from it, but a practical unity for the cause of the gospel of Christ, and for the mutual benefit of the churches. They were organized to the extent that all the churches in Greece were able to bring together their alms for Paul to take to Jerusalem (Rom. 15:25,26). They were organized to the extent that, collectively, the Macedonian churches were able to choose three men to accompany the apostle with their gifts (II Cor. 8:18-24). They were sufficiently organized to convene a council of apostles and elders at Jerusalem, to deal with doctrinal and practical problems at Antioch, problems that concerned all the churches (Acts 15). These things seem to have been achieved with very little difficulty, despite the lack of modern-day transport and communication systems.

One of the chief characteristics of Evangelical and Reformed church life in this country today, contrasting sharply with New Testament practice, is its lack of common order. One can visit a town, and search out an Evangelical or Reformed church, and enter its doors on the Lord's Day with very little idea of what one will find inside. Even two churches in the same town, bearing the name 'Evangelical', may have very different doctrinal beliefs, forms of government, and styles of worship.

This being the case, the kind of practical organization that took effect in apostolic times is no longer possible. Indeed, without there first being unity in faith and confession, it is not even desirable.

Should it not concern us that we have become so far removed from the New Testament pattern? In this country, over the last forty years, a large number of Evangelicals have taken to the lifeboats and separated from their apostatizing mother denominations, only to disperse across the wide sea of ecclesiastical and theological opinion. Each church has become a denomination of one, and as time passes we see them drifting ever further apart in faith, government, and order. Are we content with this state of affairs? Is it Biblical and God honouring?

Common concerns

There are several important, practical areas of ecclesiastical life that are of common interest and concern to all the churches, and for which a measure of organization is necessary. For many churches, particularly small ones with limited resources, it is not possible to perform these alone. Even in Independency this is recognized. The training of men for the ministry, ministerial support, and the sending and support of missionaries and their families, are three such areas. The usual solution to this problem is to resort to independent Bible colleges, ministerial aid societies, and missionary societies. Against this, however, is the complete lack of Biblical warrant for such para-church organizations. All of these responsibilities have been given by Christ to His church, and within that body He has established and recognizes just one institution: the local church. All these responsibilities, therefore, fall on the local churches as their common concern, and that necessitates their working together in federation, following the example of II Corinthians 8.

On a note of application, experience tells us that small congregations must bear far greater financial burdens than large ones, and must give more in proportion to their size for the support of the ministry. Large congregations would do well to remember this from time to time, and also their responsibility to 'Bear ye one another's burdens, and so fulfil the law of Christ' (Gal. 6:2). It is sad that small, struggling, independent churches can be left to languish on their own, with little assistance proffered by their larger, stronger, wealthier, and similarly independent neighbours.

It is at this point that we come to the nub of the controversy: denominationalism. Independency has the ascendancy at the present time because churches have rejected the principle of the denomination. But perhaps we should calmly reflect, for a moment, on the question of what is a denomination. Ideally a denomination is a number of churches, being of one mind and one voice, that voluntarily federate together to experience the same unity as that so manifestly enjoyed by the churches of the New Testament. They are churches that know and love the communion and fellowship that only a common faith and confession can give. They are churches that know the unity of the Spirit, living in peace and striving together for the faith of the gospel. They are churches that have begun on earth to reflect the perfect unity of the body of Christ that they shall know in heaven. Unfortunately, in our experience of denominations they rarely live up to that high ideal.

Denomination or church?

To dispel some of the misconceptions that often arise regarding denominationalism, it must be stressed at the outset that a denomination is comprised of churches; she herself is not the church. She is not an *ekklesia*.

The term *ekklesia* is the Greek word translated 'church' throughout the New Testament (Authorized Version), and is the source of our English word 'ecclesiastical'. It refers to 'the called out, separated congregation or assembly' of God's people.

A careful reading of the New Testament will reveal the usage to which *ekklesia* is put, and broadly speaking we find it is used in just two senses. In the first place, it can refer to the invisible church, i.e., the universal body of Christ throughout all ages, as in Matthew 16:18 where Christ says 'I will build my church' (cf. Matt. 16:18; Eph. 1:22,23; Eph. 5:23-32 and Col. 1:18,24).

In the second place, *ekklesia* can refer to the visible church, i.e., the church on earth at any one time. This second meaning can be distinguished further into a general sense and a specific sense. It is the general, or world-wide, visible church of apostolic times that is spoken of by Paul in I Corinthians 12:28, 'And God hath set some in the church, first apostles, secondarily prophets, thirdly teachers....' Also in Galatians 1:13 this general sense is in view. There Paul confesses to his readers, 'beyond measure I persecuted the church of God, and wasted it'.

But in the vast majority of cases, where *ekklesia* refers to the visible church, it is meant in a specific, local sense. As examples we may cite the following selection: 'And when they had ordained elders in every church...'(Acts 14:23); '...all the churches of the Gentiles' (Rom. 16:4);

'The churches of Christ...' (Rom. 16:16; cf. vs. 1); 'For first of all, when ye come together in the church, I hear that there be divisions...' (I Cor. 11:18); 'Unto the angel of the church of Ephesus write...' (Rev. 2:1).

The point is that at no time do the New Testament writers use the term *ekklesia* in a manner which corresponds to what we know as a denomination. It is the local congregation that is the church, the *ekklesia*. Therefore, that congregation must jealously guard her autonomy, recognizing no authority over her but the authority of Christ, exercised through elders. Many of the fears and prejudices directed toward church federation stem from painful experience in denominations that have thought they were a church, and have exercised more power and authority than was rightly theirs.

Apart from the rare occasions that we have mentioned above, the New Testament speaks of only two 'churches': the universal church of all ages, comprised of all the elect, and the church local, the latter being the visible, institutional manifestation of the former. Christ has given the ministry, the keys of His kingdom, the sacraments, and the authority to exercise discipline, to local churches, not to denominations. This is what defines the limits of denominational activity, making it wrong for a local church to surrender those Christ-given responsibilities to a denominational gathering, such as a synod. The ordination and calling of a minister, for instance, rests with the local church. His credentials should be held by that church, so only that church, not a denominational 'court', can depose him from office.

For this reason, I believe the word 'church' may not be used legitimately to describe a denomination. While it is proper to speak of a denomination of churches (plural), to speak of, for example, 'The Methodist Church' or 'The Lutheran Church', or 'The Church of Wherever' is to abuse the word, giving it a meaning the Spirit of God has not authorized.

Even if The Westminster Assembly, in its *Form of Church Government*, was right to state that the churches of Jerusalem and Ephesus were each made up of several congregations[1]—which is by no means

---

1 *The Form of Presbyterial Church Government: 'Of Classical Assemblies.'* In: *Confession of Faith and Subordinate Standards.* Free Church of Scotland, 1973 (reprint); 178-179.

proven—that does not mean that a nation-wide or even regional denomination of churches may be called 'one church'. Jerusalem and Ephesus were not large geographical regions like England, Scotland, or the U.S.A. Even if they did constitute more than one congregation, then at most we may call them city churches, i.e., several congregations under one city-wide government; but when Paul wrote to the Galatians, covering a much larger geographical area, he addressed 'the churches of Galatia' (Gal. 1:2). Likewise he refers to 'the churches of Asia' (I Cor. 16:19), 'the churches of Macedonia' (II Cor. 8:1), and 'the churches of Judaea' (Gal. 1:22; I Thess 2:14), all in the plural (cf. Rev. 1:20-3:22). Let us keep to this Biblical practice and terminology.

Denominations in history

Historically denominations have arisen largely as a necessary consequence of the church's divisions. It could be objected that we read nothing of denominations in Scripture, and that is quite true. It was to be a thousand years before the first major division took place in the church. But we do read many commands to separate from error and apostasy, and separation by its nature causes a division.

An interesting passage in this regard is to be found in I Corinthians 11:18-19: 'For first of all, when ye come together in the church, I hear that there be divisions [Greek: schisms] among you; and I partly believe it. For there must be also heresies [Greek: sects] among you, that they which be approved may be made manifest among you.' Paul is saying here that it is to be expected that divisions should occur in the church. They cannot be avoided, such being the present fallen state of human nature. Divisions are caused not by those who follow after truth, order, and peace but by the enemies of truth, order, and peace; and, painful as they are, they must take place so that 'they which be approved may be made manifest'. Here already we have a foretaste of what was to come.

For many centuries after Pentecost there was only one institutional 'denomination' of churches. Not until the year 1054, with the separation of the Eastern churches from the Western, did this situation change. Five hundred years later saw another major division with the Protestant Reformation, heralding the beginning of the fragmentation of the visible church into the bewildering multitude of denominations we find today. Of course, this does not mean that the church as an organism has been torn asunder. Such is the spiritual nature of her unity that we can always confess by faith, in the language of the Apostles' Creed, 'I believe *an* holy, catholic church.' But it does mean that her unity goes unexpressed.

On a practical level, as a consequence of this fragmentation, there is a danger that churches might lose sight of the broader picture, forgetting that the body of Christ is much larger than any one denomination. Inward looking, exclusive attitudes can develop, as easily in Presbyterian and Reformed church government as in Independency. Where churches or denominations have arisen along different historical routes, but are united in the faith, they should make every effort to establish institutional unity, so that all the churches might go forward together in the work of the gospel, to the glory of God.

False ecumenism

Any institutional unity must always be on the basis of a common understanding of the truth. In stark contrast to this, what may be called Biblical ecumenism, stands the false ecumenism of the ecumenical movement. This struck me with some force recently as I listened to a cleric speaking during a radio broadcast. He defined the ecumenical movement as a coming together of churches of *different* faiths. Biblical ecumenism, I would contend, is the expression of unity by churches of *the same* faith.

The ecumenical movement is an attempt to cover up all the historical divisions and create a single vast world-wide church institution. Whatever success it may be deemed to have by its supporters, however, the final product of all its efforts can only be a grotesque monstrosity, a caricature of the true church. Why is this? Because in its folly it has forsaken truth. Jerusalem has become Babylon, the church of the Antichrist (Rev. 17).

The only conceivable way in which the main-line churches and denominations of today can return to the true unity of apostolic days is by retracing two thousand years of history. This means taking the path of confession and repentance before God for the errors and heresies that caused the divisions in the first place, and returning to His blessed truth as it is in Christ Jesus. That they will never do.

The all-consuming drive for institutional unity at any price that we see across the world today, exposes the grave danger of seeking unity for its own sake. When the search for institutional unity is elevated above love and jealousy for the truth, it becomes an unbiblical distraction that will lead the churches ever deeper into apostasy, and will ultimately destroy them. There can be no true, God-glorifying unity without the truth. This is why the emphasis in Scripture is not on unity but always on truth. Truth begets unity. Love for the truth is first; unity follows. Unity is the servant of truth, not its master.

But however much institutional unity has been corrupted over the generations, or however bitter our own experiences of it may have been, we may not shun it. Indeed we must promote it. We must not let experience cloud our judgment or determine our church practice for us, but we must go back to the Scriptures.

We have a Biblical example to follow in the council of apostles and elders that met at Jerusalem, and whose proceedings are recorded for us in Acts 15. This chapter provides us with the clearest guidance on not only the true nature and form of institutional unity, but principally its *purpose* in preserving the churches' order and unity in the truth.

6.

The Keeping of Biblical Church Unity

III. Unity and Autonomy

The beauty of confessional unity, unity in the truth such as that experienced in apostolic times, is that the people of God enjoy a unity of doctrine and a unity of worship. Occasionally, however, unforeseen problems arise. Doctrinal controversies erupt on subjects that are not adequately covered by the churches' creeds, if at all. Examples may include marriage, divorce, and remarriage; headship; and the sign-gifts of the Spirit.

One such problem that arose at Antioch, during the time of the apostles, concerned the place of circumcision in New Testament churches. Visitors from Judea were saying to these Gentile believers, 'Except ye be circumcised after the manner of Moses, ye cannot be saved.' (Acts 15:1). This was a grave departure from the truth, adding a condition of human merit to the gospel of free grace and unconditional salvation. This is why Peter found it necessary to remind the gathering, 'But we believe that *through the grace of the Lord Jesus* Christ we shall be saved, even as they' (Acts 15:11). A more serious issue could hardly be imagined.

This dangerous teaching threatened to destroy the order and unity of the Antioch church, causing 'no small dissension and disputation' (Acts 15:2; cf. v. 7). While unity is based upon the truth of God's Word, this was a lie. This was heresy.

What is of interest, however, is that it was not left to the church at Antioch to sort out the problem by itself, even though both Paul and Barnabas were in the city at the time. Why was this? After all, Antioch was a well established, autonomous local church that had benefited for a whole year from the teaching of Barnabas and Saul, as he was then called. (Acts 11:26; 13:1). In the New Testament each local congregation is held up as a church in its own right, the body and temple of Christ (I Cor. 3:16; 12:27), accountable to Christ alone, without as much as a hint of subordination to any other, perhaps larger, church. Even small house-churches are granted the distinction of being called a church (Rom. 16:5; I Cor. 16:9; Col. 4:15; Philm. 2). In each one, regardless of size, Christ is present preaching, giving the sacraments, and gathering into and cutting off from His kingdom. As one writer has put it, 'each church, even the smallest and meanest, owes its origin and existence solely and directly to Christ and His Spirit.... Every church is, accordingly, a church of Christ, and is not a subdivision or branch of another church, be it in Jerusalem, in Rome, or elsewhere.'[1]

Why, then, was it decided by some in the church at Antioch, that 'Paul and Barnabas, and certain other of them, should go up to Jerusalem unto the apostles and elders about this question' (Acts 15:2)? Was not the apostle Paul qualified and able to deal with the situation? Indeed he was. He could have declared the truth with infallible, apostolic accuracy, settling the matter there and then, without further ado. So why the journey to Jerusalem?

The answer, I believe, lies in the unity of the church, as understood by the believers at Antioch and throughout the early church. The churches were autonomous, and yet they recognized that they were one, each being in spiritual unity with all the others. Together they made up the visible church of Jesus Christ, one in faith and confession, having one Spirit, one hope, one Lord, one faith, one baptism, one God and Father of all, who is above all, and through all, and in all (Eph. 4:4-6).

The circumcision question was an issue affecting far more Christians than those in Antioch. It threatened to drive a wedge right down the centre of the churches and re-open the age old distinction between Jew and Gentile, the distinction which Christ had for ever abolished 'in his flesh' (Eph. 2:11-22; Gal. 3:28). If the error took hold it would travel like wildfire wherever the gospel spread.

In our own day too, we do not need to be reminded that heresies and strange doctrines still spring up and have the potential to wreak

---

1 Herman Bavinck. *Our Reasonable Faith*. Baker Book House, 1977 (reprint); 534.

havoc among the churches. And some do wreak havoc. Teachers of false doctrine never confine themselves to their own little sect and neighbourhood. They go about pandering to malcontents, those with ears itching for something new, and spread their heresies wherever they can gain a hearing, disrupting the unity of the churches.

Neither is heresy something that comes into the churches only from without. It comes from within too: 'Also of your own selves shall men arise, speaking perverse things, to draw away disciples after them' (Acts 20:30).

The question is, How are we to deal with it?

The problem at Antioch was handled in precisely the manner that would be expected of churches conscious of their unity, and anxious to preserve it. Autonomous churches have a wealth of accumulated wisdom, and it is right and proper that they share that wisdom for the good of the church as a whole. Apart from anything else, it is an expression of the communion of saints.

What was at stake at Jerusalem was not just the orthodoxy of the Antioch church but the united faith and confession of all the churches. The truth on which their unity was based was under threat, hence they all had to be involved in dealing with the problem. They all must be represented at the assembly and they all must recognize its binding authority. Thereby the truth would be upheld and unity would be maintained.

It is the application of this abiding principle that is sadly missing amongst Evangelical churches today, contributing much to the ecclesiastical muddle in which we find ourselves.

In order to understand how this principle may be applied, we need to take a closer look at the events recorded in Acts 15, and see how they relate to the life and government of the churches.

We will focus on a number of key words and ideas found in the passage.

The Jerusalem Council

◆ 1. Elders

The first thing we should note is that the responsibility for deciding the issue at Jerusalem fell on the apostles *and elders*. This is emphasized throughout the passage. The question was referred to 'the apostles and *elders*' (Acts 15:2); the assembly that came together to consider it was made up of 'the apostles and *elders*' (v. 6); the decrees 'were ordained of the apostles and *elders*' (Acts 16:4). This establishes a pattern for the entire New Testament age. While it was necessary for the apostles to be present, for reasons we shall give below, it is the presence of elders that provides the key to the council's significance for our own day. Elders form the ruling body of the local church, being charged with the oversight of the flock of God throughout the new dispensation (Acts 14:23; 20:17, 28-32; I Tim. 5:17; I Pet. 5:1).

What Acts 15 is teaching us, therefore, is that when elders face a situation in the local church that they cannot resolve alone, or that concerns a matter common to all the churches, then they are to seek advice from a wider circle of wisdom. Moreover, this is to be done in a certain, proper manner. It is not to be done by means of an informal, private correspondence between elders, or friendly telephone calls, but by a formal and public assembling of church leaders.

This principle is inherent in what is known as 'Presbyterian' or, on the continent of Europe, 'Reformed' church government.

The words presbyterian and its alternative, presbyterial, are soundly Biblical terms being derivatives of the Greek *presbuteros*, meaning 'elder'. Often in the Scriptures the word refers simply to an elder person, such as the elder brother in the parable of the prodigal son (Luke 15:25), but it is also used to refer to men raised up by God to a specific office and function in the church, as here in Acts 15. The elders who came together at Jerusalem were *presbuteroi* (v. 6), i.e., presbyters. On the one occasion when the word refers to the body of elders in a local church, it is simply transliterated in the Authorized Version as 'presbytery' (I Tim. 4:14). We would do well to restore these terms to our ecclesiological vocabulary.

New Testament church government is presbyterian church government in its primitive simplicity and purity. That is to say, it is government by presbyters, i.e., elders. We do not pretend that everything bearing the name of Presbyterian today is Biblical, any more than every church claiming to be Evangelical believes and declares the true evangel, but we do maintain that churches seeking to be Biblical in their government will strive to follow the New Testament presbyterian pattern.

Recent years have seen welcome moves in Evangelical circles toward a more Biblical concept of eldership, notably to a plurality of elders in the local church. But this has taken place very much within the context of Independency. What is needed next is a formal expression of unity between churches that are one in faith and confession, with the facility to call elders together as and when needed, to oversee matters of common concern. That would constitute a welcome return to New Testament church order.

♦ 2. Extraordinary

The second feature of the Jerusalem council we should note is that it was *occasioned by a specific case*, namely, the demands of certain Jewish converts for the circumcision of Gentile believers. It is safe to assume that if these false teachers had not arisen, then what we know as 'the Jerusalem council' would not have taken place.

There is nothing in Acts 15 to suggest that the council at Jerusalem was a part of the ordinary, on-going government of the churches. On the contrary, everything seems to point to it being an *extra*ordinary gathering. The expression 'being assembled', found in verse 25, means simply that they 'came into being', or 'became', indicating that as a formal body the council had not existed prior to these events, and had no continuing authority over the churches. Thus the principle of local church autonomy was not violated.

The *ordinary* government of the churches was, and continues to be, by elders ruling in the local congregation. The Jerusalem council assembled to deal with a specific question affecting all the churches, and one that, in any case, the local church at Antioch was not able to settle (v. 2). The council, therefore, was not a standing body but a temporary assembly, existing only for as long as it was in session. It had the virtue of protecting local church autonomy, in that only issues put forward by the Antioch church itself was discussed, while at the same time providing a forum for appeal to a wider circle of wisdom. When the appeal had been made, heard, and answered, the assembly was dissolved.

♦ 3. Dispute

There was genuine debate at Jerusalem. The Scriptures tell us that there was 'much disputing' (Acts 15:7). In its Greek original, this word 'disputing' carries with it the idea of 'seeking'. In other words there was a genuine searching after truth. We may think this strange and unwarranted seeing there were apostles present, who, by a single statement, could have given the authoritative mind of God on the whole matter. That being so, why the deliberating and disputing? Without turning the entire episode into some kind of charade, there can be only one explanation. The apostles were showing, by way of example, how the churches were to behave in all similar circumstances. In the future, when issues threatening their unity arose, their leaders were to assemble, and together they were to search out the truth from the Word of God.

✦ 4. Spiritual

It may be something of a digression from our subject, but an important one nonetheless, to stress that the case prompting the convening of the council was a *spiritual* one. The apostles and elders were not concerned to pass resolutions on the social problems of first century Antioch, or the political policies of the Roman government. Their concern was solely for the church—her doctrine, and her unity.

One is reminded of an incident in later church history—the occasion in 1655 when a number of ministers in the county of Devon met to establish what became known as 'The Exeter Assembly'. Among the Articles of Association they formulated was one concerned with this very issue: 'In our consultations and debates we will not meddle with civil or secular matters, or any state affairs, nor go beyond the bound of our calling, but treat of those things only which concern us in our Ministerial function for the discharge of our duty, and seeking the spiritual good of the souls of the people committed to our charge.'[2]

✦ 5. Authority

It is essential to recognize that the Jerusalem council carried *authority*. So often it is this question of authority that proves to be the stumblingblock for us, even when the mandate for broader church assemblies is granted. The nature and extent of the council's authority becomes clear from a number of considerations:

---

2 Worth, R N. Puritanism in Devon, and The Exeter Assembly. *Transactions of the Devon Association* 1877; IX:279-280.

- i. The council was made up of apostles and elders (Acts 15:6). The objection is sometimes made that the presence of the apostles, which of course the church does not have now, made it an event unique to those times of apostolic authority, and was therefore unrepeatable. In response it is sometimes suggested that the apostles themselves were present in their capacity as elders (cf. I Pet. 5:1; II John 1), and of course elders too wield authority in the church. The Holy Ghost has made them 'overseers' in the church (Acts 20:28; I Peter 5:2). They are the church's spiritual rulers whom we are exhorted to obey (Heb. 13:17). They are over us 'in the Lord' (I Thess. 5:12), meaning that they are Christ's servants, through whom He exercises His kingly rule in the church.

However, one does not need to divest Peter, James, and Paul of their apostleship in order to establish grounds for synodical church councils. In fact, I am more inclined to believe not only that they were present as apostles, but *necessarily so*.

The presence of apostles does not make the Jerusalem council a one-off, unrepeatable event. While it is true that the church no longer has the office of apostle, it is also true that she now has the complete canon of Scripture, and while the elders met at Jerusalem with the Old Testament and the apostles, today they will meet with the complete Word of God before them. They will meet to search the Scriptures, prayerfully seeking to be guided into all truth by the Spirit. Then, when they have arrived at a knowledge of the truth, they will convey it to the churches as settled and binding 'decrees' to be received, as at Antioch, with joy (Acts 15:30-31). The authority of any such assembly, therefore, is not the authority of men but of Scripture and its divine Author, albeit mediated through men. This is the New Testament pattern. This is the pattern for us today. How closely are we adhering to it?

We should note, in passing, that the elders were not present at the council merely as spectators, while the apostles made the decisions. It was necessary for them to be there as representatives of the Jerusalem church. It was a council that was constituted *by* the churches, and with authority that came *from* the churches.

- ii. 'And as they [Paul and Silas] went through the cities, they

delivered them the decrees for to keep, that were ordained of the
apostles and elders which were at Jerusalem' (Acts 16:4). The Greek
word translated in this verse as 'decrees' is the word *dogma*, a word
that has entered the English language to mean an opinion or body
of belief, 'formulated and *authoritatively* stated.'[3] There are just five
other occurrences of this word in the New Testament, falling into
two groups. In Luke 2:1 and Acts 17:7 it is used to mean the laws
of civil rulers, and in Eph. 2:15, Col. 2:14 and Col. 2:20 the
references are to the ceremonial laws of the old covenant. The
implication is that the decrees issued by the Jerusalem council
carried at least as much weight as the decrees of the Caesars, and
even as much as God Himself in giving the ceremonial laws to Israel.
They were not to be treated lightly.

• iii. It appears that when the council had finished its work, there
was only one thing left for the churches to do: they were to *keep* the
decrees (Acts 16:4). They were not told to discuss them further at
the local church level, or subject them to a process of ratification,
but simply to keep them. The talking and discussing was over, the
decisions had been made.

The decrees were not merely advisory or recommendatory, to
be accepted or rejected as a matter of choice, but were authoritative
and binding on the churches. Indeed it was necessary for the council
to carry this degree of authority for the unity of the church to be
maintained. A mere talking shop, which produced resolutions for
further ratification, would have taken the churches nowhere. Some
churches voting to ratify, and others not, would have resulted in
total confusion and the breakdown of the very order and unity they
were seeking to preserve.

♦ **6. Submission**

Following the decision of the council, the elders and apostles, 'with
the whole church' at Jerusalem, chose Silas and Judas Barsabas to
accompany Paul and Barnabas back to Antioch (v. 22). Letters were
written to the churches in Antioch, Syria, and Cilicia, outlining the
assembly's conclusion (vs. 23-29). These, Paul and his companions took

---

3 *Shorter Oxford English Dictionary* (3rd. ed.). 1992 (reprint); I:591.

with them for the brethren in those churches to read. The reaction at Antioch is described to us in verse 31: 'when they had read, they rejoiced for the consolation.'

After spending some time at Antioch, Paul and Silas 'went through Syria and Cilicia, confirming the churches' (v. 41). We are told, 'as they went through the cities, they delivered them the decrees for to keep, that were ordained of the apostles and elders which were at Jerusalem. *And so were the churches established in the faith, and increased in number daily*' (16:4,5).

The churches recognized the council's authority and submitted to it without question. This spirit of submissiveness was evident already at Jerusalem for we are told, in the first place, that immediately following Peter's speech 'all the multitude kept silence' (15:12). The heated discussions and disputes with which the proceedings had begun were now over as the Spirit of God reigned throughout. He so worked in the hearts and minds of the antagonists that their arguments were defeated and their mouths stopped.

In the second place, although the decrees had been ordained by the apostles and elders, the private members or 'brethren' of the Jerusalem church concurred in their decisions. The letters sent were written in their name too (v. 23).

At Antioch the church 'rejoiced for the consolation' (v. 31), receiving the judgment of the apostles and elders in a spirit of happy submission. They were glad, not only that the burden of the Jewish ceremonies had been removed, but also that the disputing was now over and unity was preserved.

As for the churches of Syria and Cilicia, we do not read that any of them rebelled against the Jerusalem decision, but rather that as a consequence of it they were all 'established in the faith, and increased in number daily' (Acts 16:5).

What is the significance of all this? It is that while these churches were *autonomous* churches, they were clearly not independent. The church at Antioch was an autonomous church, but that did not stop her from referring her problem to a broader ecclesiastical assembly. The church at Jerusalem was an autonomous church, but that did not stop her from receiving the delegation from Antioch, nor her elders from entering into discussion of the problem and issuing authoritative 'decrees'. The churches throughout Syria and Cilicia were autonomous churches, but that did not stop them, together with the churches at Antioch and Jerusalem, from joyfully submitting to the authority of that broader assembly, such was their concern for unity in the truth. Autonomy does not preclude interdependence.

Of course, there were very good reasons for the churches' submissiveness. In the first place, they were submitting to God's Word. In the second place, it was the churches themselves that had called the council into being, and it was their own elders that had sat on it. In rejecting its findings the churches would have rebelled against those elders, in clear contradiction of Scripture. The responsibility of church members is to 'Obey them that have the rule over you, and submit yourselves' (Heb. 13:17), and that applies when ministers and elders meet in the churches' broader assemblies as much as when they do in the local church. As much in synod as in the session or consistory room[4] of the local church, 'they watch for your souls, as they that must give account' (Heb. 13:17).

To summarize, then, the Jerusalem council was an authoritative assembly, convened by the churches to consider a specific ecclesiastical problem referred to it by the church at Antioch. The pattern set for us, therefore, is for synodical assemblies, meeting as and when necessary—which could well be annually—to deal with particular cases that arise within the churches but that cannot be resolved by the local elders alone. However, there is no mandate in this passage for an on-going, overall governing body of the churches. The only seat of government in the church is the local eldership.

In passing, it is striking to notice the clear relationship that exists between the church's visible unity and her government. Each of the offices has its rôle to play. Where church government is soundly Biblical, unity will not be a problem but will follow as surely as day follows night. This surely highlights the importance of church government, a subject all too often dismissed as secondary, or even as one on which the Scriptures do not speak with a clear voice.

---

4 Presbyterians refer to the local eldership as the church 'session'. Literally it signifies elders 'sitting' together. The continental Reformed churches use the term 'consistory'.

Hierarchy

The example of the Jerusalem council was followed many centuries later by what have become known as the ecumenical or general councils, such as those at Nicea (AD 325), Constantinople (AD 381) and Chalcedon (AD 451). In addition to these general councils were others called by churches in particular districts to deal with problems specific to their own areas. Among these were the Ante-Nicean Councils held at Antioch (AD 269) and Rome (AD 313). Both of these were convened to consider the emergence of heresies, namely the proto-Socinianism of one Paul of Samosata, and Donatism respectively.

However, by this time in church history episcopacy had become well established. Bishops had taken to themselves more power than they possessed by right, and a hierarchical structure was beginning to take shape. The seeds of the papacy had been sown.

This leaven of hierarchy is nowhere to be found in the Word of God. It is rightly shunned and feared by all for whom Scripture is the sole authority in matters of faith and practice. There was no hierarchy in Acts 15. The only authority submitted to there was the authority of Christ as it came to the churches through the Scriptures, by the Holy Ghost, mediated by the apostles and elders. And it was because the decisions of that council were thus stamped with divine authority that they were binding on the churches represented, i.e., all the constituted churches of that time.

In seeking to restore this practice today, a number of churches that are bound together in common faith and confession as we have described will also together humbly submit to the Word of God. When their ministers and elders meet in an official capacity, representing the churches, to search the Scriptures concerning a doctrine or practice common to them all, then their conclusions will carry the authority of Christ and be binding on all those churches. That will be true even if for some reason a local church is not represented in person (cf. Acts 16:4).

But there will be no hierarchy. The authority of a synodical assembly or council is the authority of Christ in the Scriptures, and the elders present represent churches who unitedly submit to that authority.

A hierarchy is like a pyramid. The local churches form the base of the pyramid, while above them are numerous tiers of ever increasing authority until eventually one reaches the top to find the highest authority of all. This is the way in which the Roman Catholic system is structured, with the Pope at the top as its head. Quite clearly, in this kind of arrangement the local church has very little say in its government. The local church is lost under a vast weight of external authority; it has long ceased to be autonomous.

Neither, in my judgment, can Presbyterianism, as it has been historically applied, always escape the charge of hierarchy. By all accounts, this very issue caused 'much disputing' at the Westminster Assembly, which is not surprising since it was comprised of both Presbyterians and Independents. Yet, the outcome was still a structure of tiered assemblies: congregational, classical, provincial and national, each being in 'subordination' to the higher.[5] Thus it is common in some Presbyterian circles to speak of 'higher' and 'lower' church 'courts', but this terminology is as regrettable as it is unbiblical.

Needless to say, the Scriptural pattern is not of a pyramid. In Scripture the local church is always central. The Jerusalem council, and any other such assembly, can be likened to a circle formed around the church, a circle made up of all the other churches represented. It does not represent a higher authority, for there is none but Christ. Rather, it represents a broader unity. Each local church may thus see itself as at the centre, yet also represented on the concentric circles around it in the churches' broader (larger) assemblies.

Perhaps if this distinction had been made clear at Westminster during 1644, the debates would have been less protracted, the outcome more Biblical, and the ensuing course of British church history far different, following a more God-glorifying, peaceful, and united line.

Arguably the worst form of hierarchy is where one man, a virtual pope, elevates himself to a position from where he dominates all that is said and done in a church or denomination, and none is able to challenge him. Like Diotrephes of old, he loves to have the pre-eminence in the church, and will not receive the servants of truth (cf.

---

5 *The Form of Presbyterial Church Government: 'Of Synodical Assemblies.'* In: *Confession of Faith and Subordinate Standards. Free Church of Scotland,* 1973 (reprint); 179.

III John 9). But, let it not be thought that this is an inherent weakness or fault of institutional unity. It can happen in Independency as easily as in Presbyterianism. It does illustrate, however, the care with which churches must apply the principle of federation. The Word of God is careful to put in place certain checks and balances to prevent such hierarchical tendencies developing, notably equality of the offices, mutual rule of office-bearers, and crucially, the autonomy of the local church. The churches ignore these balances at their peril. One needs only to look at the problems experienced today in some Presbyterian circles to see how far from these Biblical principles they have departed, and the price they are having to pay.

An additional check on the development of hierarchical tendencies is the limited remit and authority that the churches' broader assemblies possess, namely to those matters that are of the churches' common concern. For instance, it is not for a synod or district presbytery to exercise discipline over church members, and appoint or dismiss ministers. Such matters are for the local church alone, through the oversight of her elders, her 'presbytery' (Matt. 18:15-17; I Tim. 4:14). However, there are occasions when, as at Antioch, local churches get into difficulties and find themselves in need of spiritual or doctrinal counsel, or perhaps help of a more practical nature. In such circumstances they are not left isolated, without recourse to advice, for the Lord has graciously provided means whereby fellow churches can come to their aid.

Now it may be that on occasion a church will find herself in disagreement with the outcome of one of the broader assemblies. It is appropriate therefore that there should be mechanisms for appeal and opportunity for the reconsideration of the Scriptures. However, if a church continues at odds with her sister-churches, then unity has been broken and *ipso facto* the church has separated herself from them and can play no further part in denominational life.

Obviously a church's withdrawing herself from fellowship in this way is a serious matter and one not to be taken lightly. It must be a measure of last resort, taken only when all attempts at reconciliation have failed. When it occurs, it is an occasion for much pain and sadness on the part of all concerned, but also for ongoing prayer that unity might be restored.

Finally, it has to be said that institutional unity is no guarantor of truth; but then, neither is Independency. However, Biblical institutional unity embodies the principle that 'in the multitude of counsellors there is safety' (Prov. 11:14; 15:22 and 24:6), whereas the earlier part of that verse gives a grave warning to those of an independent spirit: 'Where no counsel is, the people fall.' In Acts 15 God has given His people a clear example of this principle at work, an example that in its day established churches in the faith and increased their number daily (Acts 16:5). Our calling is to follow that example, in obedience and gratitude to the Lord, both for the good of the churches and for our own spiritual well-being as members.

Conclusion

We live in days of small things. Evangelical churches in the U.K., churches that separate themselves from the charismatic and ecumenical movements, are relatively few, usually small, and widely scattered. In such circumstances isolation can often become an unavoidable way of life. We grow used to being alone.

Moreover, such churches are invariably Independent in their government. A formal, institutional expression of unity is viewed with anything from suspicion to outright horror. Isolation can become almost a virtue.

The consequences of this are clear to see in the diversity or, it should be said, disorder and confusion that characterize the churches of our day. While each claims to identify with Biblical Christianity and to possess the truth, each is also manifestly different from the other in both doctrine and practice. Where present, fellowship is informal and intermittent rather than official and ongoing.

Hopefully the reader understands by now that this situation is far different from the one that the apostles knew. While local church autonomy is a fundamental principle that must be jealously protected, it is not the whole story. It does not present the complete picture as we see it in the New Testament. Those early years of the New Testament church provide authoritative testimony to the desirability and propriety of visible unity on a much broader scale.

According to Scripture there is no virtue in being isolated. There is no virtue in being alone and separated from one's brethren. Psalm 133 begins, 'Behold, how good and how pleasant it is for brethren to dwell together in unity!' (Ps. 133:1). To dwell in unity is good; that is, it is commendable and beneficial, something to be desired and actively sought.

Unity is pleasant. It is precious, like the sweet-smelling ointment used in the anointing of the High Priest. Just as the perfume from that holy oil was a delight to all who smelled it, so is unity to those

who dwell in it. And not only to them, but to God also, for central to
this unity is His presence and blessing as He dwells with His people
in covenant fellowship. As He blessed Mount Hermon and Zion with
life-giving dew, so will God bless those who dwell in unity. He will
command the blessing, 'even life for evermore' in His house, the
everlasting temple that is His church.

The psalmist describes those who dwell together. This is no casual
acquaintance or loose association that he is talking about. This is
'dwelling'. This is permanent co-habitation, living under one roof, in
one house. And this 'dwelling' is both good and pleasant. It is not
something to be condemned and shunned but valued and cherished
as precious and a thing of great beauty. God Himself has said so! Yet
so many of us are strangers to that beauty.

This begs the question, Why? Why are we strangers to that beauty?
If it is true that unity is both good and desirable, why is it so little in
evidence?

There is no simple answer to this question. Part of the answer may
lie in ignorance, but perhaps it lies chiefly in unbelief. The problem
is that we do not believe that there can be any goodness and beauty in
a formal church unity. Rather than keeping our eye fixed on what
God has said in His Word, we look away and form our judgment from
the ugly caricature that is the ecumenical movement. We see the
growing apostasy of the large denominations and the relentless advance
of world ecumenism and retreat into what we perceive to be the safety
of Independency.

Institutional unity does not work, we say. It is a recipe for problems
and eventual disaster. It means local churches must sacrifice their
autonomy, inevitably become involved in doctrinal compromise and
tainted with the deviations of others with whom they are associated,
and thus lose their purity. What is more, there are bound to be
dissensions and disputes. Why, then, become involved in the first place?
Independence is the better way. Independency is the safer way: it works.

All this is sheer pragmatism and unbelief. It is a denial of the power
of grace. As I have tried to emphasize throughout, believers and
churches are not united by man but by the power of divine grace.
Christ by His Spirit works unity in the hearts and minds of His people
to create a church of unparalleled beauty. Envy, jealousy, strife,

resentment, etc., all those sinful traits that cause divisions between men are naturally present in the heart of every believer and in every church, but as the Spirit of Christ works in our hearts and churches He causes us to love Him, to love His truth, and to love our fellow saints, agreeing in true faith. He makes us gracious and longsuffering toward one another, so that as new creatures in Christ we are made willing and able to dwell together in unity. Do we believe that?

Unity is all of God, and therein lie our hope and confidence, for 'Except the LORD build the house, they labour in vain that build it' (Ps. 127:1). Let us by faith look to Him to do His work in His churches, that He may make us of one mind in the truth, speaking with one voice and submitting together to the authority of Christ our Saviour and Head. To do less would be unbelief.

What I have attempted to do in this study is to set out the relevant Biblical principles as I understand them and as clearly as I know how. From a practical, human point of view the situation looks dire and the future bleak as churches draw yet further apart with the passage of time. If there is to be any attempt to restore Biblical church unity today it must be by way of a return to the truth, and a common confession with our fathers of the historic Christian faith. That means a return to the church's historic creeds and confessions. And it means a return to Biblical, Presbyterian church government.

For a great many this will involve the painful abandonment of long and sincerely held views, but only by taking these bold steps of faith can we hope to see, experience, and enjoy again that dwelling together in unity of which the Scriptures speak so alluringly, but that is so rarely known today.